D1482501

THE POWER
OF CHOICE

THE POWER OF CHOICE

EMBRACING EFFICACY
TO DRIVE YOUR CAREER

MICHAEL C. HYTER

FOREWORD BY STEVE REINEMUND
Dean of Business, Wake Forest University
Former Chairman and CEO, PepsiCo

GLOBALNOVATIONS
WALTHAM, MA

Global Novations, LLC
200 West Street
Waltham, MA 02451
617-254-7600
www.globalnovations.com

Publisher's Cataloging-in-Publication Data

    Hyter, Michael, C.

    The power of choice : embracing efficacy to drive your career / Michael C. Hyter. – Waltham, MA : Global Novations, LLC, 2011.

    p. ; cm.

    ISBN13: 978-0-9833661-1-9

    1. Career development. 2. Self-efficacy. 3. Success. I. Title.

    HF5381.H98 2011
    650.1—dc22   2011932084

The publisher offers discounts on this book when ordered in quantity. For information, call 617-254-7600.

Publishing Consultant: Neuhaus Publishing
Book Production: Jenkins Group, Inc.
Jacket Design: Yvonne Roehler and LaDonna Jones
Photography: iStockphoto/David Marchal
Interior Design: Brooke Camfield and LaDonna Jones

Printed in the United States of America

15   14   13   12   11   •   5   4   3   2   1

I dedicate this book to my children, Ashlei, Mike Jr., Donovan,
Ten, and Ace, and to my granddaughter, Donatella.
Your future is the inspiration for this book.
I love you all.

CONTENTS

FOREWORD

Throughout my career, I have taken seriously the business imperative to develop and retain people from a wide variety of backgrounds. My efforts taught me how organizations can build effective partnerships with employees to ensure that they expand their skills and contributions throughout their careers. When I became chairman and CEO of PepsiCo in 2001, I made a commitment to have the demographics of our employees—from the boardroom to the front line—ultimately reflect the marketplace. We undertook a sweeping set of efforts aimed at the recruitment, retention, and development of women and minorities. We set specific improvement goals and tied managers' bonuses to them. We worked to create an inclusive work environment for everyone. Consequently, we built a deep bench of capable, diverse professionals. We reduced women and minority attrition to a level on par with that of white men. We improved our representation of diverse employees, and we increased employees' overall satisfaction with the company.

During those years, we also achieved significant success in the market, had strong financial performance, and expanded our global reach.

A great deal of that business success was a result of our progress in diversity and inclusion. However, we did not pursue diversity and inclusion strictly because it was good for business; it was also the right thing to do. People want to work in an organization that conducts business the right way. This book shows individuals how to play their part in creating a level playing field for themselves and others.

I first became acquainted with the concepts of Efficacy at FritoLay, a division of PepsiCo. We offered Efficacy programs as part of our strategy to attract, retain, and develop a diverse cadre of talented professionals. What I liked most about the Efficacy approach was its emphasis on shared responsibility. There were many things PepsiCo was doing to support the development of its employees. However, there's a tremendous acceleration of growth when each individual fully embraces his or her role in shaping his or her career, rather than sitting back and waiting for the company to pave the way. Efficacy, with its emphasis on individuals taking charge of their own career plans, provided an excellent—and effective—platform for executing this shared responsibility.

Mike Hyter has captured the key ideas and approaches of Efficacy in this very readable and practical book. I particularly appreciate his no-nonsense treatment of the importance of relational and influence skills. There is no doubt that professionals must develop technical or "hip pocket" skills. Technical competency can't be underestimated. Professionals must know their specialty. However, there are many technically brilliant professionals in every company. Those who make the biggest mark are those who learn how to connect with others and use their influence to lead and shape the work of their organizations.

I've coached and mentored many rising professionals during my career—and continue to do so in my role as dean of the business school at Wake Forest University. I've noticed that many mentees assume that these "soft" skills are something people just have. Hyter makes it clear that building relationships and influencing others are indeed learnable competencies. By emphasizing the connection between individual development and the needs of the organization, Hyter points the way for creating a set of learning-oriented actions that increase the likelihood of securing the organizational support and endorsement required for career advancement.

This book stands out from many others that offer career advice because it acknowledges the obstacles that many individuals encounter as a result of differences in race, ethnicity, or gender. Those who have experienced these challenges will find it refreshing to have them recognized and dealt with in a straightforward manner. Over the years, I've found that individuals who accept the existence of these challenges and are willing to partner with their organizations to resolve them are much more likely to be successful in the long run than those who either refuse to acknowledge the challenges or blame the company for their existence. In other words, individuals who embrace the principle of shared responsibility, which Hyter champions in this book, tend to come out ahead.

In the fast-moving business world of today, professionals must have a lifetime passion for personal growth and development. Having a road map for that development is essential. This book provides a critical perspective and pragmatic approach so professionals can continuously expand their capabilities.

Steve Reinemund
Dean of Business; Professor of Leadership and Strategy
Wake Forest University
Former Chairman and CEO, PepsiCo

ACKNOWLEDGMENTS

Who could have known that an idea for improving academic achievement and a commitment to making a difference would turn into a practice that has positively impacted thousands of professionals and students for more than thirty years? In the early 1970s, Dr. Jeff Howard had the insight and courage to create a development experience for minority students at Harvard University to address the educational disparities between black students and white students. Efficacy was born. Dr. Howard's success at Harvard ultimately led to the founding of J. Howard and Associates, which enabled professionals in hundreds of companies to experience those same ideas and approaches. I have Dr. Howard to thank for birthing the movement, laying the foundation, and bringing together talented professionals to make Efficacy a reality. If it weren't for his leadership, many of the key ideas in this book would not exist.

I also want to express my appreciation to Marc Wallace, Audra Bohannon, and Verna Ford for making Efficacy come to life for so many companies and individuals. Marc, Audra, and Verna were among the first thought-leaders at J. Howard and Associates, and we still hear from past Efficacy participants about how significant and beneficial the experience was for their careers. Over the years, Marc, Audra, and Verna, along with all our Efficacy facilitators, have continued to expand the ideas and their application so that Efficacy could flourish. For instance, Verna added the concept of the three types of confidence—technical, influential, and relational—that has profoundly shaped how we talk about the skills that are important to navigating a career. Audra has helped evolve our understanding of the power of making conscious choices.

Making a book that captures the approaches and impact of Efficacy isn't an easy task. I could not have done this alone. Many of my colleagues—Kameelah Benjamin-Fuller, Jan Clarkson, Jorge Farias, Diane Johnson, Luisa Kurtz, Kristine Perez-Foley, and Barbara Smith—gave their support by reading the manuscript and providing feedback along the way. Kameelah also conducted some of the interviews, and Jan did an outstanding job of pulling that information into the real-world examples in the final section of the book. Barbara helped me craft the guidelines for putting Efficacy into action that appear at the end of each chapter.

I also had the support of many folks outside Global Novations. They contributed by recounting their stories—both their successes and tough lessons. They reviewed manuscript drafts and helped me bring the power of Efficacy alive. To protect their confidentiality, I'm not going to list their names here, but I hope you know who you are and what a difference you made.

I also value LaDonna Jones for her creativity in leading the effort to create the graphics and layout, but even more importantly for her perspective all along the way. The support and encouragement of Aida Diloyan, Naomi Sutherland, Cathi Rittelmann, Oris Stuart, Janet Reid, and Vince Brown has meant a great deal to me as well. Thanks to Jenny Wendel,

Clint Poole, and the rest of the marketing team for making sure the message of the book gets out to as many people as possible.

We were all spared the anguish a project like this can generate by the calm and guiding hand of our project manager, Trudy Neuhaus. She always kept us moving in the right direction. Her overall advice and editing expertise were invaluable.

Of course, I thank my wife, Tisha, for all of her patience and support during this project (and the three years of planning). I will be forever grateful.

Finally, every project like this one requires an anchor who brings it all together. Kathy Lenox was my right hand throughout this process. Kathy has been a longtime contributor to our company and a strong partner of mine on many projects over the years. Our mutual passion and commitment to Efficacy is strong and very much aligned. Her support in helping me with the writing and editing, managing the process with all of its moving parts, and keeping me on schedule has made all the difference. I can't really express in words how much her partnership has meant to me, but I'm happy to say that we got this done and it's all good! Thank you, Kathy.

INTRODUCTION

As the president of Global Novations, I have the opportunity to speak to large numbers of up-and-coming professionals—men and women who are eager to make their mark and navigate through a successful career. These individuals are hungry for practical advice about how to accomplish the goals that are important to them. Many think of themselves as—or are considered by others to be—"different" from the majority of employees in their organizations.

In talking with these rising professionals, who come from a wide variety of backgrounds and an array of industries, I encounter an interesting ambivalence about the relevance of differences in today's multicultural workforce. On one hand, these individuals are surrounded by diversity and are confident about accomplishing their dreams. According to the 2010 U.S. Census, 35 percent of the U.S. population is from a background other than White Caucasian, and 85 percent of the population growth since 2000 has come from racial minorities. The "Corporate Diversity Report," released by Senator Robert Menendez in August 2010, says that women and minorities make up 29 percent of corporate boards today. As I write, both the president of the United States and the governor of

Massachusetts, where our corporate headquarters is located, are black men—a phenomenon I never thought I would see in my lifetime.

On the other hand, in the midst of a changing population and expanding opportunities, I still hear concerns about the impact of being different when it comes to being recognized and rewarded in the workplace. Many professionals look around and don't see many individuals like themselves in senior management. They notice that their careers aren't progressing as they expected or as quickly as their colleagues'. They see others like themselves leaving the company for unclear reasons or "better" opportunities.

As these hard-working professionals make these observations—and when they encounter the inevitable challenges or setbacks of a demanding career—questions begin to emerge: Can I get the coaching and support I need to be successful, especially from managers who are different from me? Do others accurately assess my potential to contribute, or do they jump to conclusions based on my background or gender? Do I have to work twice as hard as my counterparts to receive the same recognition and opportunities? Do I have to sacrifice who I am in order to fit in? These kinds of questions, sometimes raised overtly but more often unspoken, add another level of complexity to the challenge of managing a rewarding and satisfying career.

I've wrestled with these and other questions throughout my own career. I grew up in Detroit, Michigan, during the 1960s. As a young black man, I didn't know many corporate executives. When I graduated from Michigan State University in the late 1970s, I began working as an entry-level human resources professional for a large corporation based in Detroit. At the time, I was a typical young executive who was looking to move ahead fast. I was college educated, and I worked hard. Yet even after I had two years under my belt, I felt senior executives either couldn't see or didn't value my potential. I became cynical about the company and my future with it.

In the spring of 1980, I was invited, along with twenty-three other minority professionals, to participate in an Efficacy course. I had no idea what Efficacy was. I suspected that this seminar would be remedial—something intended to "fix" black folks—and I certainly didn't consider myself in need of being fixed.

> Efficacy is the power to produce a desired effect. It is a set of thoughts and behaviors that give you the highest return on the investment of your time and effort.

What made me show up despite my reservations was that I had heard the speaker, Dr. Jeff Howard, about six months earlier. Most black leaders of the day spoke about minorities as victims—a largely white society was to blame for what we didn't achieve. Not Dr. Howard. His focus was squarely on taking personal responsibility for one's own development. He didn't talk about what was wrong with other people or what the company ought to be doing differently. He told us that our success depended upon ourselves. I was riveted by this thinking. Was it really up to me?

During Efficacy training, Dr. Howard elaborated on the topic of personal responsibility, and the meaning of Efficacy became clearer to me. *The American Heritage Dictionary* defines *efficacy* as the "power or capacity to produce a desired effect." In the context of the program, efficacy also means "a set of thoughts and behaviors that give you the highest return on the investment of your time and effort."

I was struck that the definition didn't say a good return or a high return, but the *highest* return. Efficacy was about leveraging *my* effort to maximize my development and not settling for less than I was capable of. It was about being strategic with that effort: defining what was important to me and developing a strategy that would produce the best outcomes with the least amount of wasted physical or emotional energy. Just as the efficacy of a drug is measured by weighing how well it works against its potential side effects, my efficacy could be measured by weighing my accomplishments against their cost to me or others.

Efficacy had a profound impact on me. It helped me realize that I was concentrating much of my energy on what others weren't doing right: they weren't giving me a chance, they weren't appreciating what I had to offer, and they weren't treating me as someone with a brain. Instead, I should have been focusing on the things within my circle of control and the steps *I* could take to change my situation. A key principle of the Efficacy program is, *It's not the stimulus, it's the response.* This made it clear that I could choose how to respond to my environment and people I encounter every day; I did not have to let frustration, anger, or helplessness dictate my reaction. Unfortunate and unpleasant experiences are part of life, but we can control our response. Do we react in a way that expands our possibilities and moves us toward our desired outcomes, or does our response contract our options and limit the range of support we could receive? To this day, that core principle rings in my head whenever a situation isn't progressing the way I would like it to.

I also came to understand the importance of fostering relationships with others, even those I might not like or choose to have as friends. I spent more time cultivating a "brand of excellence" with senior executives. I became much more willing to make mistakes, admit what I didn't know, and learn from my errors. Perhaps most important, I began to seek out feedback constantly—even if I didn't always like what I heard. I made a point of getting specifics—not just reassurances or vague assessments—so I could make concrete adjustments, such as changing how I interacted with people or how I delivered what was expected of me. I stopped waiting for others to discover me, and I stopped assuming that other people's biases were holding me back. Instead, I started relying on my belief in my capacity to learn and improve and become increasingly more effective in accomplishing the goals that were important to the company and to me.

These strategies opened many doors for me. Through my efforts, and with the support of some wonderful mentors and coaches, I was rewarded with a number of promotions. Ultimately, I had the privilege of becoming an officer of the company I had joined after college—a dream come true.

I never forgot the central role that the Efficacy experience played in putting me on a path to success. I kept in touch with Dr. Howard, and eventually, I left my first career to join J. Howard & Associates, a company that has since become part of Global Novations.

When I look back on my career, I realize there were many starts and stops, many lessons I wish I had learned more quickly, and much advice I wish I'd received sooner. I'm grateful to the wonderful individuals who recognized my potential and helped me learn how to navigate my career. So this book is my effort to "pay it forward" and provide straightforward answers to the questions you might face as you immerse yourself in an often confusing and challenging workplace culture. It is about how to take *informed personal responsibility* for your career. It is about how to create options for yourself, *consciously choose* what's important to you, and decide how you will achieve your goals.

There are many books with good advice for attaining and managing a successful career. However, additional considerations apply when you or others think you're different from the majority of employees. Society has made amazing progress creating more opportunities for professionals despite their race, ethnicity, sexual orientation, and gender. However, differences still create a dynamic that must be managed in the interdependent relationships that are part of any organizational culture.

For instance, if you don't receive a promotion you expected and your manager can't fully explain why, it's easy to wonder whether bias played a role. If you don't receive much feedback about your performance, it's understandable to worry whether others are making a fair and accurate assessment of your capabilities. If others in your work group seem to overlook you, it's logical to be concerned about their level of comfort with you—and the impact that might have on your opportunities. In the face of limited feedback, uncomfortable relationships, or lack of opportunity, it's natural to ask, "If I do as good a job as my majority counterparts and play by the same rules, will I be rewarded in the same way?" When you have doubts about the potential payoff of your hard work or you encounter others who question your capabilities, it's hard to sustain the effort and resilience necessary to achieve your goal.

This book is intended as an open discussion of the challenges facing professionals who are underrepresented in the leadership of today's organizations. In early 2010, the *New York Times* reported that women represent half the workforce. But according to the "Corporate Diversity Report" I cited earlier, they represent less than 50 percent of executives. Minorities are 35 percent of the overall population but account for only about 10 percent of executive managers.

In other words, in spite of the broad array of opportunities now open to all professionals, differences still make a difference. Therefore, you need to make deliberate choices about who you are and how to represent yourself in the organization you work for. Making these choices might require much work or numerous tradeoffs if your background and identity don't always square with your work culture. However, to ignore the challenge also means cutting yourself off from the possibility of reaching your full potential—*and developing yourself to the fullest is the core message of Efficacy and this book.*

Efficacy is not about becoming successful in spite of your differences or even because of your differences. It's about expanding your definition of who you are and who you can become. It's about expanding your sense of possibilities for yourself.

It's not the stimulus, it's the response.

Efficacy is about coming to believe that the career you want is within your reach—if you are strategic and disciplined in your pursuit. You're not limited by the hard-wiring in your brain or your upbringing or your last bad manager. You have the ability to develop whatever skills and capabilities are needed. It will take time. It will take some tough choices. It's likely to take multiple course corrections. But there is no doubt that you are smart enough to learn how to accomplish what's important to you. So let's take a look at what's ahead.

In the first part of this book, we explore the foundation of Efficacy. In the second part, we discuss how to develop the skills—especially the relational and influence skills—that are required to shape the kind of career you want. We also examine the factors that sometimes undermine our efforts and sap our momentum. At the end of each chapter, a summary notes the key ideas explored and provides direction for using Efficacy principles to make choices and navigate your development.

The final part of the book offers expanded examples to help you shape your reality in a way that sets you up for success. They describe a number of the most common challenges I've heard from the professionals I counsel. For example, How do I deal with a "bad boss"? How do I exert the appropriate influence to reach my goals? How do I keep my confidence up after a serious setback? How can I cultivate the sponsorship and support I need? These examples dive deeper into the strategies for managing the obstacles encountered by many women and minority professionals as they strive to bolster their credibility and stature within their work communities.

Long-term career growth is never the result of luck; it's the result of conscious and deliberate choices. My intention is that by reading this book, you will become more aware of the choices you've made to date and the options that will best serve the vision you create for yourself. By honestly looking at the impact of your decisions—what's working and what could work better—you put yourself in a position to engage even more effectively than you have in the past. In areas where you're frustrated with your career, make different choices and get a different outcome. In areas where your choices are serving you well, be open to the possibility of an even bigger vision for yourself.

We can choose to be mediocre and to let our lives be limited by others, or we can choose to find out just how great we can be. I encourage you all to choose greatness.

PART I
THE BASICS OF EFFICACY

THE REQUIREMENTS FOR CAREER SUCCESS

As professionals contemplate their potential for success, they often wonder what's required. Individuals understandably want to know which skills will best advance their careers and earn just rewards for the effort. Women and others who are underrepresented in their organizations' leadership sometimes have additional concerns: Do I have to work twice as hard because of my race, gender, or background in order to be recognized and rewarded? Do some folks get better opportunities because of who they know rather than the skills they've developed?

At Global Novations, we've researched different kinds of organizations and the nuances of their cultures, and we've found there is a consistent pattern to the career trajectory of professionals whose skills are most developed and who are most respected. Regardless of their background or experience, and whether they've worked in large or small organizations, in for-profits or nonprofits, or in traditional or cutting-edge industries, successful professionals have all built their credibility and value by developing three areas of competency:

- *Technical Proficiency.* Technical proficiency is having the operational and analytical skills required to do a job. It refers to a person's capability to do a job accurately, reliably, and efficiently, whether it's a highly process-driven set of responsibilities, such as issuing invoices, or a highly creative one, such as designing a new ad campaign. Individuals who are technically proficient are knowledgeable about their field of endeavor and are able to do their jobs with a high degree of excellence in order to succeed. If these professionals hadn't made the effort and commitment that enabled them to be very good at their jobs, there's little likelihood they would have been offered the opportunity to do more.

   However, the mistake many professionals make, especially women and minorities, is to believe that technical proficiency alone guarantees they'll be recognized and rewarded. After developing a foundation of expertise in a field, professionals have to learn how to use that expertise in a manner that mobilizes others to act on their ideas. This is why the next two areas of competency are as important as technical proficiency.

- *Relational Proficiency.* Relational proficiency is the capability of professionals to relate to others and have others relate to them, whether or not they like each other. Organizations are made up of individuals who are expected to work together effectively. Because most people prefer to work with others they know and feel comfortable with, professionals who have developed relational skills, who can navigate across a wide variety of people and circumstances, tend to be the most sought after.

- *Influential Proficiency.* Influential proficiency is the capability to engineer mutually satisfactory solutions to problems. It requires the skills to sell ideas and to navigate an organization effectively in order to get things done. Individuals who can shape outcomes and engineer the engagement of others add more value to the organization than those who bring technical proficiency alone.

Professionals must be technically proficient in order to be credible. Nevertheless, relational and influence skills tend to differentiate individuals who experience the greatest growth and satisfaction in their careers from those who are perceived as good, but not stellar, performers. This is because organizations' expectations of individuals' contributions change over time. After professionals master the technical requirements of their role, the organization looks to them to influence the work of others and do more to advance the business's objectives. Technical proficiency is the foundation; relational and influence skills are the keys to sustaining momentum over the arc of a career. (See Figure 1-1.)

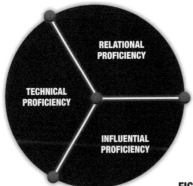

FIGURE 1-1: The Skills Required for Long-Term Growth

These three fundamental competencies are the secret sauce of success and should be the focus of your development as a professional. Let's look a little more closely at each of these requirements.

TECHNICAL PROFICIENCY

Mastery of the requirements of your job is critical. Your career will come to a standstill if you do not develop a reputation as someone who can be counted on to produce results. You need to consistently and predictably deliver what is expected of you. Then you need to go one step further. You need to be known for being excellent at something important to the business. You want your name to come up when people are looking to solve a problem or take on new initiatives. Few opportunities and little support from others will come your way unless you show that you are someone worth investing in. Conversely, doing a good job—even in something seemingly trivial—is what creates the *possibility* of additional responsibility and additional reward.

I learned this lesson about the importance of doing a good job early in my career, although I admit that at the time it was more about keeping my sanity than making a strategic move. One of my first tasks as a newly hired human resources employee was to prepare data from manual personnel records for transfer to a new computer system. I was shown to a closet-sized room with no windows and one glaring overhead light. The room was piled high with dusty manila folders. My job was to go through the information in each folder and fill out a template for the computer technicians to use in data entry. Accuracy was of the utmost importance.

It was pure misery for me to sit for long hours and focus on these painstaking details. Furthermore, I was insulted by the assignment. This was boring clerical work, not an assignment fit for an aspiring executive.

As a survival tactic, I devised challenges to get through the day. How many records could I complete in an hour? Could I finish more today than I did yesterday? How could I reduce my error rate?

Later I discovered the value of my strategy to make the work interesting. I completed the task in about half the time the company expected, so it was able to move up the timeline for computerization of the personnel records. That got me recognized by the HR leaders as someone who worked hard and delivered excellent results. The job also helped me learn the names and expertise of people across the organization—knowledge that helped me make valuable connections as I moved on to other responsibilities.

What opportunities do you have right now to be first rate in what you are doing, even if the task seems initially mundane or unimportant? How do your responsibilities contribute to the work of the business? I recently heard a radio interview with a young man who was responsible for loading pallets of roofing tiles into trucks for delivery. He reported that his job was "one of the most important ones in the company." The interviewer quizzically asked why; many of us wouldn't characterize truck loading as a critical job. The young man confidently replied that he was the last person who touched the roofing tiles before they went to the customer, so he was the one who ensured that customers got only quality tiles, not ones that were cracked or damaged. This was a man who clearly understood the value he brought to the business.

The more you understand how your work is connected to the organization's purpose, the easier it will be to figure out what you need to do well and how you can do it more effectively. Without such technical proficiency, the options you can command for yourself will be severely limited.

Technical Proficiency Is Not Enough

Although technical proficiency is necessary, I am continually struck by how many of us have been socialized by our families, our education systems, and even companies' professional development systems to believe that hard work and credentials are *all* that matter. Our parents, teachers, and mentors were right to tell us to go the best school we could, get good grades, and then do a good job in our chosen careers. Credentials get us in the door, and solid job expertise establishes our credibility. But technical proficiency isn't enough to earn us appreciation or get us promoted.

I have met with countless young men and women with impressive credentials and solid work experience who are upset and frustrated because they haven't moved up. Inevitably, they tell me that they've been passed over for opportunities that were given to others with less noteworthy credentials or less time in the position. When I press further, the issue is almost always that these individuals have spent their time working hard—very hard—but they have not invested enough effort in influencing the work of colleagues and getting to know others outside of the small circle they work in every day. As a result, decision makers tend to see their capabilities as limited to where they are currently working. And they lack the sponsorship to be tapped for opportunities outside their current work environment.

I recently counseled a young Asian-American woman I'll call Joy. Joy worked for a well-known consulting company as a tax consultant. She had an Ivy League education and worked sixty to seventy hours a week as a matter of course. In her group, she was recognized as the go-to person for questions about tax law. She recognized the need to broaden her expertise if she was going to be considered for leadership positions within her organization, and she was outspoken about her frustration at being assigned to the same client with the same demand for long hours and little development opportunity. Joy was particularly bitter that a white male peer, whom she saw as being much less capable, had just been reassigned to a highly visible client engagement.

It's tempting to look at this situation and cry foul given Joy's depth of expertise and impressive work ethic. However, as we talked more, I learned that Joy seldom delegated work to others on her team. She told me, "I've learned that if a job is going to get done right, I have to do it myself. My reputation rests on my work, and I can't risk letting someone else mess things up." When I asked if she interacted with anyone other than her client and those on her team, she said, "Given how much work I have, I have to prioritize how I spend my time." As her frustration grew, she was also vocal about her belief that "this company promotes incompetence."

Let's look at this from her leaders' point of view. What incentive is there to promote someone who works tirelessly at her current level and who has demonstrated limited capacity to support and develop others? Furthermore, she comes across as cynical and bitter about the organization in general.

Joy was correct that others with less impressive credentials and time on the job were getting promoted. She made the mistake of believing that her expertise should speak for itself and automatically lead to expanding career opportunities—and that if it didn't, discrimination was at the root of her failure to advance. What she didn't see was that she had not provided any basis for her leaders to trust her with positions where she would influence and manage others. In addition, she had few connections who could provide access to additional opportunities and champion her candidacy.

In most organizations there are many technically proficient individuals. Who gets stretch assignments, special projects, or promotions generally involves the more subtle—and to some, controversial—components of relational and influence skills.

RELATIONAL PROFICIENCY

The second important area of professional development is relational proficiency: the capability to relate to others and have them relate to you. Imagine, for example, that you are heading up a project and you can hand-select your team. Wouldn't you be more likely to choose individuals you knew you could work with well? Wouldn't you want a group that you believed would accomplish its mission with a minimum of tension and discomfort?

It's human nature to prefer working with people you're familiar and comfortable with, which is often easier to do when you think they're "like you." It can be terrifying to walk into a room where there are few others like you. It takes courage to introduce yourself to a group of executives, especially when they are different from you in ethnicity or gender. It can be awkward to create those connections when you don't share a common background or culture. It can be disconcerting to realize that others are uncomfortable with you. For too many people, this discomfort means they avoid making the contacts and connections that could help build their careers. Instead of figuring out how to relate, they write off these relationships as too difficult or not worth the time. Then, unfortunately, they wonder why opportunities go to others.

As difficult as it can be to muster up the courage to reach out to others, it is an absolute requirement to invest in creating relationships with others. Success is never achieved single-handedly. You need people to champion you. You need a network that you can go to for advice and support. Commit to learning how to be socially graceful in a wide variety of circumstances, formal and informal, and at all levels of the organization, entry level through senior leadership. When you make the effort, you're likely to find that there are many individuals who are eager to connect with you.

Three years into my first job out of college, I attended a number of meetings where the company's chief financial officer spoke to the group. CFO was a really big job to my young eyes. In addition, this fellow had been working in the company for a long time, had a larger-than-life personality, and was widely revered. Despite our being in a couple of meetings together, he would pass me in the hall and never say hello.

One day, after attending a company-wide meeting where this CFO spoke about the current quarterly results, I felt compelled to approach him. I went up and introduced myself, acknowledged how much I appreciated hearing from him as a young professional, and said I would love to meet him again some time to become better acquainted. I was shocked to hear him say, "That would be nice. I'll have my secretary give you a call to arrange it."

To my surprise, she called me later that same day to schedule a personal meeting with him for the following week. I recall going up to the fourteenth floor where the corporate executives had their offices. His office manager met me, offered me coffee, and walked me into his big office. We spent an hour getting to know each other, sharing stories about our backgrounds and opinions about the company. A relationship was born that grew and lasted for years. His mentorship was invaluable as my career progressed.

A few years later I asked him why he agreed to meet, given how low I was on the organization chart. He said, "Because you asked me. No one else at your level had ever asked to meet with me, and it impressed me that you would." He also shared that he enjoyed getting to know me and as he learned more about me, it made him more aware of how he could support my dreams.

It was at that moment when I realized the significance of building relationships at all levels of the organization. Such relationships help build your understanding of the culture, how things get done, and what you have to do to add value. Relationships allow you to be present in the minds and actions of others. They expand the number of individuals who represent you in critical conversations about your contributions and potential. I know my company seriously considered me for opportunities because of the CFO's support. And he was better able to assess how I could add value because he was familiar with my skills and capabilities. Who would be willing to support your development if you reached out to them?

You don't have to like someone to interact effectively and in a manner that can support your goals. About ten years into my career, I attended a panel discussion about diversity. One of the speakers was a woman named Emily who had recently been promoted by a man who had a reputation for discounting the potential of women and for making inappropriate remarks about them. This was at a time when many organizations considered such behavior something women had to put up with from men of a certain generation, rather than a behavior to be overtly curtailed.

During the panel discussion, Emily spoke favorably of the support she had received from this man and how he had helped advance her career. A woman in the audience discreetly asked whether the panelist had encountered any of this boss's questionable behavior. Emily replied matter-of-factly that she had experienced some "interactions that were typical of the man's reputation." The woman in the audience became more strident at this point and asked Emily rather pointedly how she could be complimentary of a man who clearly had a derogatory opinion of women. Wasn't she selling out?

Emily's response has stuck with me ever since. She replied calmly that she realized this man was a gate she had to get through. She could regard him as a major obstacle to her advancement, or she could find a way to work with him. She decided she had more to gain from looking for the possibility of collaboration than she did from judging him. Emily explained that once she was intentional about establishing a working relationship with him, she was able to see that they had some things in common: they were both committed to the business and driven to succeed. As it turned out, her boss was a good mentor, and he was savvy about how to navigate the organization.

Emily acknowledged that not everyone would choose to draw the line where she did. However, once she decided to find a way to partner with her manager, she could put her energy into moving her career forward and working productively rather than being frustrated by a "bad boss." She also had more credibility in influencing her manager's opinion about her and about other women when he saw her as an ally and not an antagonist.

I've often thought about that story, how we often choose to be righteous rather than effective and fail to establish relationships that could benefit our development. I've noticed how we often put down others who establish connections to benefit their careers. I've watched individuals or groups be suspect of those who forge relationships with others outside their group and accuse them of "selling out" or "becoming one of them." Why limit ourselves to alliances only with those we view as most like us? Why waste some of our potential because our talents and contributions aren't known and supported by a wide variety of people? What opportunities do you have to expand your relationships and relational skills? Who might you be missing as a possible partner in an endeavor that's important to you?

The development of relational skills is critical—perhaps even more critical than becoming technically proficient. Like the development of any skill, these take time and effort, but the payoff is mutually beneficial relationships with people who will champion you and your goals.

INFLUENTIAL PROFICIENCY

The third necessary area of professional development is influential proficiency: the capability to shape opinions, inspire action, and successfully navigate the formal and informal processes of an organization. Influentially skilled people understand how systems work. They leverage situations and manage relationships to achieve desired outcomes. They position themselves and their ideas to elicit the support of others.

Influential proficiency is an area that is often undervalued and derided as brown-nosing. People are criticized for playing politics. Yet those who can sell ideas, shape opinions, and engineer mutually satisfactory solutions to problems bring more to the table than those who are only technically proficient. Wouldn't you rather partner with someone who can secure the necessary resources or provide challenging learning opportunities instead of someone who is knowledgeable but ill-equipped to make things happen? Wouldn't you prefer to work for a leader who can influence a team to work together productively rather than one who is merely an expert in the field? Wouldn't you rather surround yourself with individuals who will advocate for you? Securing resources, bringing a project to fruition, guiding a cohesive team—all these things require influence skills, and most of us want to be involved with others who can exert this kind of leverage.

The capability to influence situations, outcomes, and people increases your value to an organization. When you have the capability to do your job well, your value equals that of your independent contribution. When you are also effective in understanding what motivates others and can increase their engagement and productivity, your value equals your contribution plus theirs. (See Figure 1-2.) Mastering the art of influencing others, regardless of their level or rank, differentiates the average from the great.

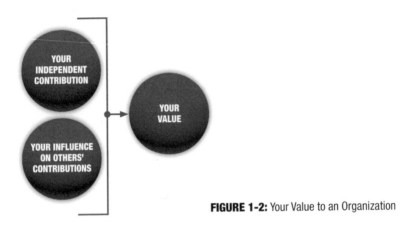

FIGURE 1-2: Your Value to an Organization

Yet many professionals assume that they have to have a high-level title or many direct reports before they can or should exercise influence. As a result, many individuals miss opportunities to develop the influence skills that enable them to accelerate their careers. They don't offer their good ideas because they're not the ones in charge. They feel they have to put up with unreceptive bosses or difficult work groups. When you can look at challenges as opportunities to improve influence skills rather than as situations outside your control, you are much more likely to figure out approaches that will persuade others to adopt your point of view or create more productive working relationships.

A successful senior executive told me that his most valuable career lessons were learned in positions where he had responsibility but no authority. To be successful, he had to figure out the motivation that would induce each individual to support his recommendations. He had to look for common interests and frame his arguments in a way that would be most likely to influence each individual. He couldn't lean on hierarchical advantage to force compliance.

Almost all positions afford opportunities to learn how to influence others. Perhaps you want to convince others to go along with a process change or shape the entry of a new person into your work group. Maybe you have a recommendation for a new product or service, or you have a suggestion for enhancing an existing one. These are all good opportunities to practice influencing others.

I recently spoke with a young supervisor in the distribution warehouse for a consumer goods company. He had been assigned to a committee tasked with finding ways to reengineer some of the company's processes; the company wanted people who actually did the work—and this fellow was one of those people. This young man couldn't understand why he was on this committee. He wasn't sure he'd have any suggestions, and he was concerned he'd end up rubber-stamping the ideas of more senior members of the group. He was convinced it would all be a waste of time and asked me how he could gracefully decline.

I encouraged him to stick it out, enjoy the visibility it offered, and look for ways to actively participate. He didn't have to position himself as a leader or as an expert, simply as someone invested in contributing. I suggested he start by looking for clues to each person's short- and long-term interests relative to this project. What did each of them envision as the benefits to the company if the group was successful? What were the personal and professional benefits each envisioned attaining? What was each person's point of view? What information did he have access to, given his position, that the other members of the group didn't?

He took my advice and adopted a new outlook. He not only looked for clues at meetings but he also went out of his way to have at least one discussion with each member outside the formal meetings. People got to know him as an individual, and he grew in his understanding of how they thought and what was important to them.

There was a moment when he recognized an opportunity for an improvement with one of the processes but still wasn't sure whether he had credibility with the group. I watched him muster the nerve and confidence to strategically position his idea in the context of what he had learned about the other members of the task force and how it could contribute to the outcomes mentioned by many of them. He was amazed to see people respond so favorably to an idea he proposed. Eventually, a version of his idea was implemented. Imagine what that did for his confidence—and his standing in the company.

I've found that many professionals from a variety of backgrounds initially balk at this emphasis on relational and influence skills. After all, technical skills are easier to measure and evaluate. Organizations place a lot of emphasis on technical skills when outlining required credentials or explaining the rationale behind certain promotion decisions. Yet, in practice, the more subjective relational and influence skills often determine who is given new opportunities. When you choose to develop these skills, you have more control over your own career. You're better able to create momentum and make a bigger impact.

Relational and influence skills are so important to career success that I've devoted entire chapters to them. Chapter 6 is about how to develop meaningful connections based on trust and shared objectives. In Chapter 7, I offer guidance on how to develop the influence skills that allow you to shape your reality rather than react to it.

WHAT'S REQUIRED FOR SUCCESS?

In summary, as you make choices about how to manage your career, it's important to consider the requirements for success. Organizations today expect you to develop technical skills and then expand your impact by connecting with and influencing others. After you've mastered your position's core requirements, your larger contribution will emerge from your capability to access and orchestrate a wide network of resources and expertise that you can bring to bear to meet the needs of the organization. The organization will look to you to shape the work of others and to do more to advance the business's objectives.

The good news is that relational and influence skills are learnable. No matter what assumptions you've made about your capability to be a socially graceful or compelling personality, you can become more adept at making connections and mobilizing the minds and actions of others. It will require your effort and attention. It will require practice and making some mistakes along the way. The payoff, however, will be a wider network that you can tap for support—on your own behalf and on behalf of your organization.

ADOPT KEY IDEAS

- Technical proficiency is absolutely required for career success. The most highly valued people in today's organizations also develop the relational and influence skills to interact effectively and shape the work and opinions of others.
- By developing all three areas of proficiency—technical, relational, and influential—you can increase your options and engineer the career that is most satisfying to you.

BEGIN NOW

Take this short assessment and consider your current level of technical, relational, and influential proficiency. Then choose one or two areas in which you would like to further develop. Take advantage of as many opportunities as possible to deliberately practice these skills.

Technical Proficiency
The operational and analytical skills required to do your job

RATE THE EXTENT TO WHICH YOU . . .	SELDOM			ALWAYS	
Are viewed as a go-to person to get the job done	1	2	3	4	5
Take the initiative to keep yourself current and up to date on the state of the industry or technology	1	2	3	4	5
Consistently maintain high quality standards for your own work and outcomes	1	2	3	4	5
Actively seek solutions to technical, process, or work-product issues	1	2	3	4	5

Relational Proficiency

The capability to relate to others and have them relate to you

RATE THE EXTENT TO WHICH YOU ...	SELDOM				ALWAYS
Put others at ease and make them feel comfortable	1	2	3	4	5
Effectively build rapport with people at all levels throughout the organization	1	2	3	4	5
Make the time to get to know others, find common ground, and build solid, professional relationships	1	2	3	4	5
Build and maintain a strong professional network in which you have support and support others	1	2	3	4	5

Influential Proficiency

The capability to shape opinions, inspire action, and successfully navigate the formal and informal processes of the organization

RATE THE EXTENT TO WHICH YOU ...	SELDOM				ALWAYS
Are successful in getting others to listen to your ideas and follow your recommendations	1	2	3	4	5
Represent your accomplishments and contributions appropriately to the right people in the organization	1	2	3	4	5
Navigate effectively though the formal and informal processes in your organization to make things happen	1	2	3	4	5
Secure the resources and support you need to accomplish your desired outcomes	1	2	3	4	5

LEARN MORE

The Three Areas of Proficiency Self-Assessment provides a more in-depth assessment of your current level of technical, relational, and influential proficiency. It also includes suggestions for how you can develop further in each of these areas. You can download the assessment from *The Power of Choice* website (www.powerofchoice.net).

BELIEVE YOU HAVE
WHAT IT TAKES

You are capable of learning whatever is necessary to achieve your goals. You are capable of becoming the person you dream to be. When you embrace this belief at your core—at an emotional level, not only a cognitive one—you are better able to sustain the commitment and motivation necessary to engineer your vision. You're able to lean into the challenges inherent in crafting the life you desire. You know that your capacity to learn what's required isn't limited by your hard-wiring. Your development is determined by the nature of your effort—by what you do to stretch yourself. Your growth is governed by what you learn from your experience.

As you navigate the increasing challenges of an advancing career, profound belief in your capacity to learn can be hard to sustain. I've been struck by how often even the most accomplished professionals confess to having moments of doubt about some aspect of their abilities. Time and time again, folks who have received that sought-after promotion have confided, "I'm not sure I've got what it takes to make it at this level." It's one of those dirty little secrets none of us likes to talk about. We put on a good front, but how often do we drive home wondering if we're smart enough or tough enough or skilled enough to succeed in some new challenge that has surfaced in our jobs?

What's the root of this phenomenon? What causes accomplished individuals to harbor doubts about their abilities in some situations? Why are otherwise confident professionals sometimes stymied by a sense of limitation at critical junctures in their careers?

THE FIXED-CAPACITY MINDSET

Our doubts about our ability to succeed can be traced to the pervasive and underlying belief in our society that some people have "it"—mental and emotional intelligence—but most people don't, or at least not in abundance. We've been socialized to believe that each of us has some collection of natural gifts and talents. Some of us are smart. Others are natural-born leaders. Still others are inherently creative. Conversely, we assume that each of us has innate limitations—and that there is little we can do to overcome them.

The belief that learning capacity and important job-related abilities are permanent, unchanging characteristics is called a fixed-capacity mindset. (See Figure 2-1.) In this way of thinking, professionals with a high capacity for learning ("naturally smart people") will be able to master the increasingly complex demands of their careers. Individuals with less capacity will eventually tap out; they will reach their "level of incompetence," and by virtue of their limited innate ability, they will find it very difficult—if not impossible—to develop the level of expertise needed at the more demanding levels of responsibility.

FIGURE 2-1: The Fixed-Capacity Mindset

With a fixed-capacity mindset, failure is viewed as evidence that a job or task is beyond a person's ability. Since ability is a permanent characteristic, the person who can't do it now probably won't be able to learn to do it in the future either. From an early age, others judge our level of mental and emotional intelligence. By the time we reach adulthood, most of us have internalized these assessments and accepted the assumptions about our natural gifts and talents and about those areas in which we can't quite measure up.

Awhile back, our firm consulted with one of the world's premier research facilities. All the scientists had one or more advanced degrees from top educational institutions, years of experience, and multiple patents. We had assumed that at this elite research institution, we would find folks with considerable confidence in their potential for high levels of performance. Yet even here, these highly competent, highly educated PhDs were often demoralized when they suspected that colleagues had gotten more challenging projects or made more significant breakthroughs because they were "smarter," more capable researchers. It reminded us that the fear of reaching the limits of one's potential affects everyone—even some of the most proficient individuals in the world.

This fear is a consequence of a fixed-capacity mindset. It primes us to be on the lookout for our shortcomings. When we spot them, perhaps because we've experienced a few disappointments or are challenged by the demands of a new opportunity, we're susceptible to believing our natural abilities have played themselves out and that we've arrived at our personal limit. It seems logical then to avoid working in situations that require those skills. Why waste time and effort in an area where we believe we are doomed to inferior results?

A fixed-capacity mindset is destructive to our confidence and inhibits our efforts to learn and grow. It feeds insecurity. And most significantly, *it is an inaccurate way to think about our potential for growth and development.*

THE CAPACITY-BUILDING MINDSET

Research in brain development and skill acquisition increasingly confirms that a capacity-building mindset is a more accurate way to represent the potential of human beings to learn and grow. A capacity-building mindset holds that human capacities are not fixed. Most people can rapidly develop new skills and capabilities; they can learn to be highly effective at a variety of complex and challenging new tasks. Sustained involvement in challenging tasks and regular practice of new and difficult skills stimulate the development of capabilities. In other words, learning is based on what the Efficacy program calls *effective effort*, not fixed abilities. (See Figure 2-2.) That means just about everyone can learn whatever is necessary to do his or her job, contribute to the organization's objectives, and prepare for increased levels of complexity and responsibility *if* he or she applies effective effort to meeting the challenges.

FIGURE 2-2: The Capacity-Building Mindset

We assume we have to learn to drive a car by getting behind the wheel and practicing. Job-related skills are no different. We have to work at them, make mistakes, and use the lessons we learn to become more expert. The more we practice, and the more opportunities we have to learn, the more developed we will become.

In their Freakonomics column titled "A Star Is Made," which appeared in the *New York Times Magazine* on May 7, 2006, Stephen Dubner and Steven Levitt focused on Anders Ericsson, a professor who studies Expert Performance, the science of examining what makes individuals good at what they do. As the authors explained, Ericsson's research demonstrates that practice and effort—not innate ability—are the key differentiators in levels of accomplishment. For example, one of his first experiments involved memory. He trained people to hear and then repeat a random series of numbers. The ability to memorize is often assumed to be a function of innate intelligence rather than a learnable skill. Ericsson showed that subjects could learn to remember more than eighty numbers. This feat took about two hundred hours of training per participant, but the capacity to learn how to remember such a long string of numbers had no correlation with standard intelligence tests, only with the type and duration of training the subjects received.

In this same article, Dubner and Levitt discussed Ericsson's discovery that a large percentage of the world's elite soccer players were born in the first three months of the year. What impact could birth date possibly have on the development of outstanding soccer skills? Ericsson noted that the cutoff for age-based youth league assignments in most countries was December 31. So children born in the early months of the year had more time to develop their muscles and physical coordination by the time player selections were made—they were almost a year older than the children born late in the year. These bigger, more mature players were more likely to get selected for the most competitive teams beginning in early grade school. Dubner and Levitt made clear what effect that has: "Once chosen, those January-born players are the ones who, year after year, receive the training, the deliberate practice and the feedback—to say nothing of the accompanying self-esteem—that will turn them into elites."

Even something that on the surface appears to be a function of innate ability—a high level of soccer-playing potential—turns out to be a function of practice and effort. Older players have had more time to develop coordination and to mature physically. Then, because of their inclusion on the most demanding teams, they get more practice competing at the most challenging levels of play. The more rigorous the training, the more developed the player.

In his research, Ericsson credibly demonstrated in a wide variety of fields—chess, golf, surgery, stock-picking, and software design—that deliberate practice (or what we call effective effort in our Efficacy seminars) is the most significant factor in determining one's level of development. Regardless of the perceived level of innate ability at the beginning of a learning process, those who become the most capable are those who set specific goals, study the feedback they receive, and concentrate on incrementally improving their strategy or technique over time.

EFFECTIVE EFFORT DRIVES DEVELOPMENT

I can't make this point strongly enough: *You have enough ability to develop in whatever areas are important to your success.* What it takes is your commitment and willingness to apply effective effort. Development comes from being devoted to the practice of improving yourself.

Effective effort is much more than working hard. Effective effort is directed and strategic. It's marked by three characteristics. (See Figure 2-3.)

FIGURE 2-3: The Three Characteristics of Effective Effort

- *Tenacious Engagement.* To develop your skills and abilities, you have to commit fully to learning. You have to be willing to give your time, discretionary energy, and thoughtful observation to the process. Simply put, you have to engage in getting better.
- *A Focus on Feedback.* Every situation in which you are involved teaches you something. Study your results. What happened? Why did it happen? What feedback and coaching can you get from others? What does all this information tell you about how to improve?
- *A Strategy for Improvement.* Use the feedback you receive to set priorities and formulate a strategy for developing your skills and talents. What do you need to do differently in order to be more effective?

We often overlook—or even discount—the impact of focused effort when we're confronted with differences in skill proficiency. A chess master typically has been playing for ten years, often four to six hours a day, from a very early age. Such a player has had significant opportunity to study patterns in moves and to learn to anticipate the impact of certain strategies. Certainly he or she will be much more proficient than the casual chess player who plays a game or two a month. The difference is time and effort rather than innate intellectual ability.

We also don't consider that the "numbers genius" in the finance department spends hours studying complex spreadsheets and so learns to see the patterns and trends. And we don't take into account that the "natural-born leader" might have started bossing her younger brother around when she was four years old, honed her skills as president of her high school class, and went on to form a new club in college. We look at her in her first job and label her as a natural leader. Unfortunately, neither she nor those around her fully understand that her leadership skills were years in the making.

I have seen the impact of focused effort and practice in my own life. When I began making presentations to groups, I did a mediocre job. Speaking to fellow professionals and executives was a new undertaking for me, but I was overly confident in my interpersonal skills. I thought I could show up, notes in hand, and impress the audience with my insights and charm. Instead, people listened politely, but I didn't create a lot of buzz, and people didn't come up to me afterwards to learn more or continue the conversation.

At first, I was tempted to ignore the audience reactions that were telling me I needed to do a better job. Then I realized that a colleague, Corine, was getting much better reviews than I was. The reason? When Corine was scheduled for a major presentation, she set up several internal opportunities to practice. During those sessions, she asked for the group's insights and questions about the topic and adjusted her presentation based on their input.

Corine also reached out to the communications experts in our company and asked for coaching. She received suggestions for how to stand, make eye contact with the audience, and use her PowerPoint slides more effectively. Her tenacious engagement and voracious use of the feedback resulted in her rapidly becoming a more effective public speaker.

I realized that if I was going to accomplish my career goals, I needed to improve my presentation skills. I began scheduling my own practice sessions, requesting coaching, and incorporating the advice I received. Gradually, I became a much better keynote speaker. I continue to be amazed when someone calls me a natural at public speaking when nothing could be further from the truth. It was practice, practice, practice.

I encourage you to look at those areas where you might be settling for an average or even mediocre level of expertise because you have come to believe that your talents lie elsewhere—or because you have been unwilling to commit the effort required. What difference might it make if you were to engage more fully, look for more opportunities to practice, and focus on strategies for improvement?

I'm not saying that there are no differences in capability. There are some third graders who read better than others. There are professionals who can repair a piece of equipment more quickly than their peers or make a more compelling presentation. Rather, my point is that your current level of capability in any arena is not predictive of how much further you will be able to develop. Many slow readers in early grade school become accomplished, intellectually adept professionals. Many senior executives in charge of millions of dollars in revenue were once considered average students. Many shy individuals learn the art of relationship-building and exert broad influence in their fields. The variable is their incremental efforts to improve over time. In his book *Outliers*, Malcolm Gladwell repeatedly mentions the "10,000-hour rule," claiming that the key to success in any field is, to a large extent, a matter of practicing a specific task for 10,000 hours. Whether or not 10,000 hours is the right figure, the point is well-taken: differences in levels of development are largely a function of the quality and quantity of effort, much more so than the level of innate talent. If you're willing to immerse yourself, learn from your mistakes, and improve over time, you will become proficient.

FAILURE AND DIFFICULTY AS FEEDBACK

One of the most striking differences between the impact of a fixed-capacity mindset and a capacity-building mindset is how each way of thinking affects our use of the feedback required to grow and learn, especially when that feedback comes in the form of a failure or setback.

When you have a fixed-capacity mindset, you interpret a failure or difficulty as evidence that you don't have what it takes to be successful in a particular area. (See Figure 2-4.) You then avoid working on those tasks that require the expertise you don't have—and believe you have little potential of learning. Soon, failure becomes a kind of self-fulfilling prophecy: you believe that you lack ability in some area, you avoid working on tasks where that lack might be exposed, and you don't improve because you have no opportunity to learn from your mistakes and improve the effectiveness of your effort.

CAPACITY-BUILDING MINDSET
- Our potential is unlimited and depends on effective effort
- Failure provides information on how to improve
- We seek opportunities to learn
- We engage to discover solutions

- Our potential is limited and unchanging
- Failure indicates lack of ability
- We seek opportunities to demonstrate ability
- We avoid risk and ambiguity

FIXED-CAPACITY MINDSET

FIGURE 2-4: The Impact of the Two Mindsets

In contrast, when you have a capacity-building mindset, a failure or difficulty provides information about *how to improve*. It's the gold you mine to determine what you need to do differently. If your proposed layout for an ad campaign is rejected, you don't say, "I'm a bad graphic designer." Rather, you assess—and, ideally, ask others to assess—which elements of your design might have been effective, which fell short, and why.

The psychological shift is huge. In a fixed-capacity mindset, failure and difficulty are embarrassing, even shameful; they expose inadequacies we believe we have little ability to improve. In a capacity-building mindset, difficulty has a much different sting. It might be frustrating, it might be temporarily embarrassing, but it's also information about how to improve. The feedback directs and focuses our effort; it helps us make our approach more effective. It doesn't tell us to stop working, and it certainly doesn't confirm any permanent limitations.

Fixed-capacity reasoning sets up a damaging Catch-22 around the need to work hard at something and our willingness to practice diligently. In fixed-capacity thinking, one of the indicators of "natural ability" is ease of execution. If we can perform a task easily—if we can analyze a set of numbers quickly or ad lib a presentation without much advance preparation—then we assume we have a natural talent in that area. If we have to work hard and put in long hours to be effective, it's seen as an indication that we're not naturally talented in this area. It's no wonder then why it's hard to muster the motivation and perseverance to learn something new when the effort only reminds us that we don't quite measure up.

To make matters worse, if we avoid working in some area, our estimation of our ability becomes true over time. Our skills stagnate and we don't develop new competencies. However, this underdevelopment is not because of any innate lack of ability. Rather, it is because *we avoided the very challenges that allow us to learn new skills*—an unfortunate consequence of a fixed-capacity mindset.

I was reminded of this recently when I went to visit some old friends, Rose and David, both of whom have been successful automotive sales-people for years. During 2009, many auto dealerships saw their revenue drop as a result of the 2008 financial crisis. Sales fell as customers tightened their belts and decided that buying new cars was more of a luxury than a necessity. Like other sales folks, Rose's revenue numbers declined. But then they leveled off, and almost as soon as the economy saw early signs of recovery, Rose saw her sales start on an upward trend again.

I was struck by the contrast between Rose's experience and that of my friend David. David's sales took the same initial hit, and they continued to decline slowly, even after the economy began to recover. The contrast made me curious. Here were two very capable and effective salespeople. Why did they have such different experiences? Why had the turbulent economy been so much more difficult for David?

As I discussed the situation with each of them, it became apparent that David had never quite believed in his ability to sell cars. He inherited a well-developed dealership from his dad and in his words, "just kept it going." He was shaken by the severity of the crisis and the challenges the economy posed. He quit calling his clients regularly, because he reasoned that they didn't have money to spend and he didn't want to pressure them. Since he was no longer involved in regular discussions with his clients, his level of engagement changed. His intentions were good, but by failing to ask himself how he could alter his approach given the changed circumstances, he lost two opportunities: to expand his skills and to help his clients.

Rose told me that at first she had a similar reaction to David's. Why call her clients if they were holding the purse strings tight? But then she realized that her clients needed her partnership. Their needs hadn't gone away; they just couldn't afford the same level of cars and servicing as in the past. So Rose continued to check in regularly with her clients about the problems they were facing. She was unsure about what would work, but she assumed she'd find solutions for her customers as she continued to interact with them.

This level of engagement provided Rose with information that David didn't have because of his less frequent interactions. Her clients shared information about their automobile-related needs and those of their friends. Rose partnered with some of her clients to find ways to unload autos that were costly to maintain in favor of more gas-efficient cars. She focused on low-cost maintenance services that kept older cars running longer. She sent customers articles with gas-saving driving tips. All these strategies kept her connected with her clients and immersed in their problems. Her approach positioned her to make the business case for new cars when her customers were more secure with their respective employment and more confident that the economy would improve.

Both sales professionals faced the same challenge: a down economy that necessitated different customer strategies. David doubted his capacity to rise to these external challenges and withdrew from the client interactions that could have helped him determine how to be effective in the changed circumstances. Rose, on the other hand, assumed she could figure out some way to address the challenge. She stayed engaged and by doing so received feedback and information that helped her shape how she could serve her clients. She learned more by staying in the mix than David did by sitting on the sidelines.

Is something similar going on with your development? Notice your reactions when you're faced with some new challenge. Do you feel your energy expand? Are you looking forward to mastering the challenge?

If your answer is yes, it's likely you're operating from a capacity-building mindset: you believe you are capable of learning and this challenge is an opportunity to expand your skills.

If you feel your energy and effort contract, however, and you move away from the challenge, you're probably operating from a fixed-capacity mindset.

For many of us, it is tough to fully accept that we are capable of learning whatever is required to respond to a challenge or reach our dreams. But I encourage you to choose to believe in your potential for greatness. Pick one area where you want to grow and develop. Engage fully in learning, study the feedback you get from your own experience, and zealously ask for feedback from others. Then apply what you learn to improve incrementally. You're likely to be amazed at just how good you can be.

ADOPT KEY IDEAS

- You have enough mental capacity to develop high-level professional skills. To learn and grow, you need to apply effective effort.

- Stretch yourself to learn something new, study the feedback you receive from your experience, and apply what you learn to incrementally improve over time.

- Failure and difficulty are not indications of any permanent lack of ability. Rather, they provide feedback about how you need to refine the nature of your effort.

BEGIN NOW

- Identify an area where you are confident in your capacity to perform well. How have you developed this level of expertise? What has supported your confidence so that you could develop in this area?

- Now think of an area where you are less confident in your capacity to be effective. How is your effort and level of engagement in this area different from the one in which you have more confidence in your capabilities?

- Tell yourself that you are capable of improving in this area. If you let yourself believe this, how could it impact your willingness to engage in tasks that will support your learning? What specific actions could you take to learn and grow in this area?

LEARN MORE

Take the Mindset Assessment to gain greater insight into the degree to which you tend to operate from a fixed-capacity mindset and from a capacity-building mindset. You can download it from *The Power of Choice* website (www.powerofchoice.net).

Mindset: The New Psychology of Success is a wonderful book by Carol Dweck. Dweck is a social psychologist and professor at Stanford University who has spent her career studying the two mindsets. She offers practical advice for building what she calls a "growth" mindset.

THE POWER
OF THE MESSAGE

In spite of all the progress we've made in becoming a truly diverse society, there are still lingering questions—spoken and unspoken—about the abilities of certain groups. Can professionals with strong accents relate effectively to clients? Can women make the tough calls that are necessary at the highest corporate levels? Can professionals of color lead effectively in traditionally white organizations? At one time or another, most of us have had to confront stereotypes like these in order to secure the opportunities and recognition we deserve.

Having to prove we are capable and committed can be frustrating and draining, but the greater harm happens when we let others' doubts creep into our psyches—when we begin to seriously question whether we're smart enough or bold enough or creative enough to attain our goals. Internalizing those doubts begins to undermine our confidence, and when that happens, our development is at risk.

Almost all of us can recount a situation where our abilities were questioned and the doubts affected our mindset and effort. I have a particularly painful and striking example from early in my career as a human resources manager. I felt I had conquered the demands of my position at the time, and I was eager for more challenges and new responsibilities. So I was excited when Bob, my vice president, announced he was recruiting for a new director-level position. I thought this was a chance to advance my career.

I still vividly remember discussing the opportunity with Bob and the sting of being told I was "intellectually weak" and didn't "have the bandwidth for the job." He told me that my current position was the peak of my potential and that he expected me to assist him in recruiting and hiring the director who would eventually become my new boss.

I was devastated. And I accepted that what he had said to me was true. I began forgetting simple tasks. I was reluctant to speak up in meetings for fear of appearing dumb. I began to question whether I was cut out for corporate life. Every day was a struggle to get out of bed to come to work, and I felt pretty defeated about where my life might go.

Fortunately for me, Bob was fired and replaced by Susan, a vice president from our corporate finance department. Susan had never worked in the human resources division before, so the first thing she did was to reach out to her direct reports to ask for our collective experience to assist her in building the best department possible. I remember thinking, "She assumes I have something to offer." With just that little acknowledgment of my value, it got easier to get out of bed in the morning.

Susan also revealed that she was aware of my interest in the new director position and didn't want to make a decision until she had given me an opportunity to demonstrate my capabilities. She even went one step further: she reassured me she'd partner with me to develop the needed skills. I can't tell you how awesome I felt after that meeting. Not only was Susan giving me a chance, but she was actively supporting my success.

Susan was true to her word. She took the time to explain the big picture behind her decisions. She asked me for my perspective. She gave me assignments that stretched me and increased my visibility among other senior executives.

As you can imagine, my confidence returned with this kind of partnership. Coming to work was fun again. I worked doubly hard to be effective, and I did everything in my power to aid her success in her new role. You should have seen the tears in my eyes when I was promoted to director six months later.

As I think back on my experience now, I'm struck by the realization that I had the same set of talents and potential when Bob chopped away at my belief in myself as I did when Susan positioned me for success. The difference was that I let Bob's assessment of my abilities destroy my confidence and undermine my efforts. For a while, I let his negative expectations determine who I was and how I performed. His messages hit some vulnerability in me at a time when there weren't a lot of young black men in corporate America and I was still struggling to establish myself and ground my professional identity. I often wonder where my career would have gone if Bob hadn't been fired.

I've heard countless stories like my own. Some professionals recount a positive ending; others are still struggling to let go of negative beliefs they've internalized about themselves, sometimes going back to childhood. It is inevitable that we will experience some level of difficulty when we're stretching ourselves to take on new and demanding challenges. And it's inevitable that we will experience some level of judgment and doubts from others. We can't control the assumptions others make about us, but we can control the impact of these messages. We can be intentional about how we respond when others expect less of us than we are truly capable of. My dream is for no one to be dependent on a manager like Susan appearing on the scene to perform at his or her best.

A DOWNWARD SPIRAL

Here's the pattern that typically emerges when someone overtly or subtly raises doubts about our abilities or expresses low expectations in an area where we're vulnerable: The doubts and low expectations erode confidence and undermine our efforts. Because our effort is compromised, our performance is less likely to be satisfactory, which confirms the original low expectations—in our minds and in the minds of others. (See Figure 3-1.) The cycle can then become self-sustaining because we've internalized the low expectations of our capabilities. Even after there's no longer a Bob in the picture, we doubt ourselves and our capabilities.

Doubts and Low
Expectations

Diminished
Confidence

Ineffective
Effort

Compromised
Development

FIGURE 3-1: The Downward Spiral

Low expectations are seldom as stark as those that I received from Bob. Usually, they are more subtle, but they can be equally capable of damaging your belief in yourself. Your manager might ask who helped you with a project or why you think you can lead a team. Other times, you might detect doubt in a colleague's voice, notice that you're not considered for opportunities as regularly as your peers, or observe that few professionals like you have been successful in a particular role or at a particular level of leadership. Sometimes it's just the feeling of invisibility; no one notices you. You have the title but not the authority; people make decisions without you.

Some of the negative messages you receive might even be well-intentioned. Family or friends advise you not to take a promotion and "avoid all that stress." Or colleagues tell you to pass on a challenging opportunity because "it will never get you anything but trouble." These types of counsel might be intended to protect us from disappointment or failure, but they nevertheless convey a negative assessment of our potential for success.

Sometimes negative external messages have minimal impact. We become frustrated or angry that we have to address them again and again, but overall, they don't affect our confidence in our capabilities or our commitment to developing them. Other times, we are vulnerable. We remember a parent or teacher who doubted us. We recall a past failure or difficulty. We focus on some problem we're currently having and wonder whether the low assessment of our ability could be true. Or perhaps at some level we've absorbed the stereotyped messages. The result is that our confidence in our ability to be successful is compromised. We start to doubt ourselves.

When we begin to wonder whether others' doubts about our abilities could be true, the resulting anxiety and tension impede our best efforts. Think about the contrast between situations where you were confident that you could be successful and those where you were fearful of failure. In which circumstances were you able to harness your highest level of creativity and energy to solve problems and achieve your goals? Although there are some folks who do their best when they are called on to prove themselves, most of us experience a high level of anxiety and tension, which is at best a distraction and at worst a self-fulfilling prophecy. We're no longer excited by our work. We find ourselves avoiding certain kinds of tasks; we pass on an opportunity.

Low expectations can cause people to worry about failure, compromising their effort and ultimately, the outcome.

I was reminded of this when a colleague of mine was agonizing about her ten-year-old son's batting slump in Little League. He'd had several at-bats where he missed the ball and struck out. At first, he was disappointed. But now his fear of not hitting the ball had begun to overwhelm his ability to react to a pitch. He was stuck in a downward spiral: strikes produced anxiety, which crippled his ability to perform, in turn producing more anxiety and more strikes. And because he was in a slump, the coach wasn't playing him as much since he couldn't count on him to get a hit.

Low expectations can create the professional equivalent of a batter's slump. Our focus is divided between worrying about failing and actually working on the challenges of the situation. So our effort is compromised—and ultimately so is the outcome.

Then, faced with less than stellar performance, we have to explain our lack of success. We've already been primed to view the situation as one where there's some deficiency on our part. So we're likely to confirm in our minds the initial negative expectations we received from others. The downward spiral is now complete: we've internalized the original low expectations.

ALBERTO'S DOWNWARD SPIRAL

I saw this downward spiral play out with Alberto. Alberto is a Venezuelan man in his thirties. When I began coaching him, he confided that he feared his accent interfered with his ability to communicate—and would prevent him from advancing in the company. As I got to know him, however, I never found his accent to be an issue. In fact, in our one-on-one conversations, he was engaging, and his command of English was excellent.

One day, Alberto told me his manager had asked him to make a presentation to a senior executive group. His manager broached the subject by saying, "I know you find it difficult to make presentations because of your accent, but I think it's important you give this talk. You know more about this topic than anyone else on the team." I'm sure the manager meant to be supportive, but he touched on one of Alberto's biggest fears: that his communication skills would lead to his being judged negatively by senior management.

We decided to practice together for the presentation. During our first session, Alberto was noticeably nervous, spoke quite rapidly, and was indeed difficult to understand. I suggested some techniques for remaining calm, because when he relaxed, he spoke more clearly. In spite of our practice, on the day of the presentation, Alberto was extremely nervous and spoke too quickly. When members of the executive group asked him to repeat a few points, Alberto's manager jumped in and said, "I know it might have been hard to understand what Alberto was saying . . ." This unnerved Alberto to such a degree that he withdrew from the conversation and his manager had to carry much of the discussion around the presentation.

Understandably, Alberto was devastated. When we debriefed, he said, "I'm not good at presentations. My accent is just too strong, and I get too nervous. I'm going to tell my manager that someone else should give these presentations in the future." His confidence was badly shaken. But more importantly, he no longer thought it was a situation he could change and was losing his determination to try.

Notice the big leap from not doing as well as he wanted on this presentation to not giving any more talks. That's often a consequence of negative expectations; they cause us to amplify the impact of a single failure into something more global. Rather than saying to ourselves, "I messed up this one opportunity," we magnify the significance to something more catastrophic: "I don't have what it takes to give effective executive presentations."

Undertaking a task and failing might be embarrassing or dispiriting, but giving up is not the answer. By avoiding assignments or situations that require us to stretch and improve our skills, we forego opportunities to become more proficient. When this becomes our modus operandi, over time we become less accomplished than others who embrace opportunities to learn and grow. In turn, our limited skill set confirms the doubts that others—and we ourselves—have about our abilities.

CREATING AN UPWARD SPIRAL

How do we break this downward spiral and create an upward one? How do we maintain the confidence we need to pursue our development? In short, by embracing the capacity-building mindset—the belief that we can learn any skill, provided we use failure as feedback and invest effort to improve. (See Figure 3-2.) A capacity-building mindset makes us less vulnerable to external questions about our capabilities. It allows us to focus on the effort required to learn and develop new skills.

Ongoing
Development

Effective
Effort

Improved
Confidence

Belief in Capacity
to Learn

FIGURE 3-2: The Upward Spiral

I helped Alberto make a more objective assessment of his communication skills so that he could more accurately say to himself, "Day to day, I communicate effectively. However, when I'm nervous, I speak too quickly, and it's hard for others to understand me. I need to practice the strategies that help me be at ease in front of a group. I need to remember to speak slowly." I encouraged him to look for new opportunities to practice his presentation skills rather than prematurely closing doors. Given his current level of anxiety, it would be ideal if Alberto looked for opportunities to do some additional practice in front of groups where there is less riding on the outcome. Once he builds up his confidence, he can take on the executive group again.

Giving up or avoiding challenges destroys confidence and stalls the process of development. When you ask yourself what you need to do to improve and then design an incremental process to get better, it increases your confidence and builds your sense of control. You've identified the problem and have a plan to correct it. The more you develop, the stronger you become, and the more resilient you are when faced with the low expectations of others. The greater your awareness of the dynamics created by low expectations, the better you can intervene to shore up your confidence and reinforce the effort required for development.

Consider one great example of a national accounting firm successfully interrupting the downward spiral of a group of employees and creating an upward one. The company had laudably committed itself to the long-term goal of increasing the number of people of color among its partners. Its first step—to recruit a more diverse group of recent graduates to fill entry-level auditing positions—was successful. However, these newer hires were passing the CPA exam at significantly lower rates than their white counterparts. The company began to wonder about its decision. Was it recruiting at the right schools? Was it choosing the right candidates? Underneath these concerns was the unspoken but most damaging question, Were individuals like these (in this case, predominantly black and Hispanic employees) intellectually up to the rigors of the profession?

The firm engaged Global Novations to assess the situation. During interviews with the new hires, we discovered several things. They understood they were being closely scrutinized, and they knew they were considered by many to be "affirmative action hires." They had observed that there were few "like them" in leadership positions, so they were unsure of the likelihood of their success. Additionally, they suspected management was raising questions about their abilities since few were passing the CPA exam.

Facing such headwinds, these new recruits experienced an understandable drain of confidence, motivation, and commitment despite their previous records of academic success. Many of the recruits were not consistently participating in study groups or other programs designed to support them, nor were they negotiating with their managers for time to prepare for the exam or using personal time, such as vacation days, to study.

Each reported feeling anxious about his or her prospects. In addition, each assumed he or she was the only one having doubts. When we asked why they weren't taking better advantage of the available resources, they first told us about their busy schedules and client conflicts. However, as we dug a little deeper, many acknowledged that they feared being "found out." Should the firm discover the degree of difficulty the exam presented, their inadequacy would be exposed.

We recommended that the company become more forthright with these employees. It should let them know that the CPA exam is a demanding test, the programs the company sets up are not remedial but are valuable and necessary support structures, and everyone who is studying for the exam should take advantage of all available resources. Most important, it should convey to these recruits its confidence in their abilities; the company wouldn't have hired them otherwise.

During the first two years of the accounting firm's program, fewer than half of the new hires passed the exam. At the beginning of the third year, after the company took steps to more strategically build confidence and convey high expectations, everyone passed. The combination of overt expressions of belief in the trainees' capabilities, acknowledgment that the test is challenging for all professionals, and greater accountability for using the resources available resulted in more effective preparation, mutual support, and, most significantly, passing grades.

CHOOSE THE UPWARD SPIRAL

You can't eliminate stereotypes and low expectations. You can, however, become more aware of how these subtle messages affect your confidence and your commitment to develop your abilities. Awareness gives you greater choice in how you respond. Will you succumb to the low expectations of others or choose to believe in your potential for learning and development?

Often, the first signal that low expectations have affected your self-confidence is that you avoid or procrastinate on some task. You might even devise a variety of seemingly reasonable explanations for your behavior. You tell yourself that the challenge in front of you really isn't an area of interest, it's not important to your advancement, or you don't have time. If you're serious about your development, get serious about realizing when you're making excuses or rationalizations rather than confronting your fears and pursuing your development.

> Ask yourself if you're making excuses rather than confronting your fears and pursuing your development.

Over the years, I've asked many groups about their behavior when they are questioning their capacity to succeed. According to one group, at such a time they are most likely to:

- Stay busy but never find time for the things that are most critical
- Avoid the project or withdraw
- Tell themselves their family needs them and they shouldn't take on a new opportunity
- Not take any risks and play it safe
- Take unrealistic risks so they can't be blamed if they fail
- Dress, talk, or act in a way that puts others off
- "Stay the kid" rather than assume responsibility
- Avoid feedback and deny that there areas in which they need to improve

One of the women in the group even confided that she had four children—each five years apart. Every time her youngest child was entering kindergarten, she acknowledged that she would contemplate returning to the paid workforce. Although the prospect of returning to work excited her, it also scared her. So, in retrospect, she realized she resolved the issue by becoming pregnant. Certainly with a new baby on the way, it was no time to face the uncertainty of a new job.

Deciding to have a baby, turn down an assignment, or stay in the same job is not necessarily an indication that you're avoiding a challenge, but it could be. If you're serious about advancing your career and going after what's important to you, be intellectually honest with yourself. Are you making excuses for why you're not investing fully in some endeavor when in reality you're doubting yourself or fearing the possibility of failure? Such misgivings are normal; we all experience them. However, you can choose how you respond. Will you let your possibilities be driven by others' low expectations and your own fears? Or will you take the risk of engaging in challenging opportunities that feed your growth and development?

Each of us has to decide what we want to accomplish and make decisions and choices that honor those goals. We all have to develop the emotional and intellectual resilience to confront stereotypes, embrace new and challenging tasks, and risk failure. We have to trust that we can develop the skills necessary to be successful in whatever endeavors we undertake. For only by making a strong commitment to our development and taking those risks can we develop the skills that prove to ourselves, and others, that we have the capacity to be the person we dream of being.

ADOPT KEY IDEAS

- It's not the stimulus, it's the response. Regardless of what others say or do, your power to engineer your desired outcomes rests on how you respond.

- Be on the lookout for signals that low expectations are eroding your confidence or compromising the effectiveness of your effort.

- Don't let others diminish your belief in your potential to develop. Be willing to risk engaging in challenging opportunities that grow your capacity.

BEGIN NOW

- What messages have you received, directly or indirectly, about the possibilities for people "like you"?

- How have these messages affected the decisions you've made in your life? Have they had an impact, for example, on the opportunities you've tried or those you've passed on, or the responsibilities you've gravitated toward or avoided?

- Are there any areas where you feel you've limited your options because of the impact of these messages?

- Now that you're more aware of the effect of these messages, what expanded choices might be available to you? How could you take action to expand your development?

LEARN MORE

Where Have I Been? Where Am I Going? is a self-assessment that helps you identify patterns in the life and career decisions you have made. Do you proactively move toward your goals or move away from challenge and risk? Are your decisions driven by confidence or fear? Greater self-awareness of the drivers of your decisions supports you to be more intentional in your future choices. You can download this assessment from *The Power of Choice* website (www.powerofchoice.net).

PART II
CHOOSE YOUR STRATEGY

BUILD CONFIDENCE

Difficulty is inevitable—even necessary—in the course of your career development. In order to grow, you must test your skills in new areas. Sometimes you will do well, and sometimes you won't, but what ultimately determines your success is how you respond to these challenges. Do you learn from your mistakes? Or do you see them as indications of your inadequacy and retreat from your goals? If you learn from your experiences, you'll develop more confidence, which will help you to be forgiving of yourself when you experience difficulty and enable you to stay engaged in moving toward goals that are important to you.

There's an implication to the meaning of confidence that is significant. In general discussion, many of us use the word *confidence* to mean that I believe I can accomplish a particular task or goal now—at this moment. Efficacy expands that definition to include the belief that *I can learn* how to perform a job or achieve an objective, even if I can't do it now. Believing you can learn is the true essence of confidence. It would be nearly impossible to have confidence that you could currently accomplish everything. However, having confidence that you can learn incrementally opens up a wide range of possibilities. It offers the motivation necessary to commit yourself to endeavors, to trust that you will learn what's required to succeed over time, and to persevere until you reach your goals. Confidence based solely on what you can accomplish now is limited. Confidence based on the belief that you can learn is boundless.

> Confidence based solely on what you can accomplish now is limited. Confidence based on the belief that you can learn is boundless.

Confidence is what drives effective effort, which is the basis for long-term development. And your effort becomes effective when you put yourself in situations where you learn from your experience. When you believe in your capacity to improve, you soak up the feedback that allows you to learn. True confidence predisposes you to ask yourself, What information can I take from this experience that will enable me to be more effective the next time? How can I improve my effort and my outcomes? Whether you succeed or fail, every experience teaches you something about how to engage more effectively the next time. Your expanding expertise in turn reinforces your confidence and improves your results. The cycle becomes self-reinforcing.

Two factors are critical to building robust confidence. The first is self-talk: what you tell yourself about why you succeed or fail. The second is the support of those around you. You have significant control over both of these factors. Let's start with self-talk.

SELF-TALK

Self-talk is that inner dialogue we have with ourselves about why we had the outcomes we did. It tends to be very different from the discussion we have with our managers or peers about our successes or failures. It's the conversation we have with ourselves in the quiet of the car or train ride home: Did I get lucky? Was it because I worked hard? Did I succeed because I had good support from others? Did I fail because my manager is temperamental or because I'm not very smart?

How we answer these questions profoundly affects our beliefs about whether we can achieve the same or better results the next time around. A key strategy for building confidence is to become more aware of the explanations you give yourself about success and failure so that you can be more intentional in your self-talk.

Self-Talk After a Success

Think about a project or task you completed successfully although you were unsure you could accomplish it. You probably had some anxiety at the outset, but you were able to succeed in spite of whatever obstacles you encountered. What did you tell yourself about why you were successful? For most individuals, explanations generally fall into one of four categories: luck, external circumstances, ability, or effort. The self-talk in each of these categories affects your confidence differently. (See Figure 4-1.)

FIGURE 4-1: Self-Talk After Success

Luck and External Circumstances

In the first kind of self-talk, luck, we might say to ourselves, "Whew! I was lucky I pulled that one off!" In other words, we chalk up our success to chance. In the second type of self-talk, external circumstances, we explain a success in terms of the task or external environment. For example, we might say the job was easy, anyone could have done it, my team really supported me, the audience wasn't very critical, or I was successful because I have a great manager.

When you tell yourself you successfully performed a challenging task because you were lucky or it was easy, how likely is it that your success is going to raise your confidence that you can be successful the next time? After all, you can't rely on being lucky, and you can't always count on external factors, such as your team's support. So when you explain a success in terms of luck or anything outside your control, the success doesn't help build your belief that you can repeat it. The success doesn't reinforce your conviction that you are someone who can learn how to accomplish challenging goals. Confidence increases only when your explanations for your outcomes support the belief that you can repeat the success or even take on something more challenging in the future.

This kind of self-talk is one reason many successful individuals don't feel confident. They don't own their successes; they don't take credit for what they've done. Although it is true that sometimes circumstances *do* work in our favor, you can't lose sight of what you contribute. An uncle of mine used to say, "Luck is where preparation meets opportunity." Few people are successful based on luck or external support alone. It's great to acknowledge the conditions that facilitated a success or to congratulate your team for the role they played in a project win, but you also have to acknowledge, at least to yourself, the value of your own efforts.

I've mentored several professionals who were reluctant to take on a new opportunity because it would separate them from a manager who had nurtured and guided them. Although a good mentor or coach certainly contributed to their success, these individuals undervalued their own efforts to make the most of their managers' mentorship and gave too much weight to their managers' support. As a result, they had too little confidence that they could learn to be equally successful in a new setting.

Ability and Effort

To build and sustain confidence, it's critical to acknowledge the role of ability and effort in your self-talk about success. When you explain your accomplishments in terms of your abilities, you acknowledge, for example, that you succeeded because you're smart, talented, or experienced in a particular area. When you explain your success in terms of your effort, you credit your preparation, strategy, or approach. For example, you might tell yourself you succeeded because you worked hard or smartly, you devised a good strategy, or you understood how to sell your point of view to the right stakeholders.

Notice that these two explanations—ability and effort—are about you; they are factors within your control. Therefore, they are much more likely to build confidence. They also are much more accurate: you succeeded because you are capable and used a good approach. Self-talk focused on ability and effort increases your sense of control. Your ability isn't going to vanish, and you can repeat your effective approach.

Own Your Successes

The first step in building confidence is to own your successes. Tell yourself that you succeeded because you are a capable individual who made the effort and used the right approach to reach your desired outcome.

Then, analyze your success, being as specific as possible. Don't just tell yourself that you did a good job. Identify the behaviors that led to your success. How did you prepare? Which approaches worked well? Then ask what you learned that you could apply in the future.

For many of us, owning our successes runs counter to messages we received growing up about being humble and not getting a big head. We were taught not to take our accomplishments too seriously. For example, a number of studies have shown that women are more likely than men to explain away their successes by crediting their teams. I'm not suggesting you become arrogant or dismissive of others' contributions, but giving proper weight to your own accomplishments—and your potential for continued growth—establishes an important foundation for confidence.

Self-Talk After a Failure or Difficulty

For most of us, the most vulnerable time for our confidence is after a failure. I'm using the term failure broadly to refer to all situations where our outcomes aren't at the level we desire. I'm not referring only to those few dark moments when we've made a serious mistake. I'm also talking about those circumstances where the results aren't quite up to our own or others' standards or the impact falls short of our goal. Although we might not think of such situations as failures, we do have to explain the gap between the outcomes we would have liked and the actual results.

The explanations for failure fall into one of the same four categories we already discussed. However, after a failure, the self-talk is a little different. (See Figure 4-2.)

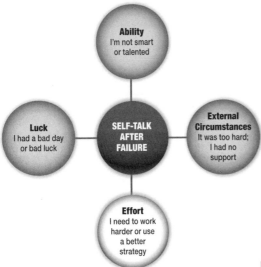

FIGURE 4-2: Self-Talk After Failure

Ability

Telling yourself you failed because you lack ability is probably the most damaging and limiting kind of self-talk. When you're engaging in an inner dialogue, this self-talk usually begins with such phrases as, "I've always had trouble . . . ," "I'm not the kind who can . . . ," "I'm not good at . . . ," or "I never could . . . ." You'll notice that this kind of self-talk generally comes from a fixed-capacity mindset. It's rooted in a belief that you don't have the ability to accomplish a particular type of task and you're not likely to have it in the future.

External Circumstances and Luck

Explaining a result in terms of the task or other external factors is also common after a failure. In this case, individuals often use reasons such as, "It was too hard," "My manager didn't support me," "It was an unreceptive group," or "The process was faulty." They might also attribute a failure to having a bad day or bad luck.

Faulting external circumstances and luck are less damaging to your ego. They remove the sting that comes with blaming yourself for a lack of ability. However, they do little to *build* your confidence that you could get better results the next time around. It might be true that the expectations were unrealistic or that the process was faulty, but if your self-talk stops there, it's unlikely the experience will expand your sense of control or increase your confidence in the possibility of engineering a better outcome in the future.

Remember, one of the key principles of Efficacy is, *It's not the stimulus, it's the response.* Self-talk focused on external circumstances or luck emphasizes the stimulus. It draws our energy toward what is being done *to us* rather than toward the possibilities for improvement or greater control. To build confidence and direct our attention toward a useful response, it's important to explain our failures in terms of something we can change going forward. *The only thing we can change is the nature of our effort.*

Effort

When you explain your failure in terms of effort, your self-talk focuses on the strategy or approach you used. This type of self-talk begins with thoughts such as, "I didn't work hard enough," "That wasn't the best method," "I didn't really understand all the pieces that were important for success," and "The next time around, I need to do this differently."

Explaining your failure in terms of your effort puts you in control. You can work differently; you can apply what you learned. You can work to improve a faulty process. You can influence the support of others. Explaining your failure in terms of your approach—the nature of your effort—reinforces the belief that you have the ability to create a different outcome in the future.

Some self-talk about the nature of our effort is, in reality, disguised judgment about our lack of ability.

A word of caution: some explanations people give themselves appear on the surface to focus on the nature of their effort, but in reality, these reasons are disguised judgments about their lack of ability. "I should have done better" is a comment I often hear from those I counsel. What these individuals mean, however, is that if they were more capable, they wouldn't have made a particular mistake. Telling yourself you failed or had difficulty because you didn't use the right approach is different from *blaming yourself.* Be analytical and curious about what you can do differently after a failure, but don't beat yourself up.

I also hear people remark that they need to put in more effort. But again, what they are really telling themselves is, "I'm not really that smart, so I have to work extra hard." Anything challenging requires hard work. The need to work hard at something is *not* a reflection of your potential, it's information about your current level of development. You might be at a different stage of development from someone else, but remember, any challenging endeavor requires significant effort in order to learn to be proficient.

Learn to tell yourself that failure or difficulty is only information about how to improve your effort and get better results—and believe it.

Failure Is Feedback

Given how fragile our confidence can be, this idea bears repeating: failure is feedback; it is information about how to improve. Failure is *not* an indication of your worth. It's not a confirmation of your lack of ability, and it's not a prediction of your future potential. It's only data about those areas where you need to do more learning and growing. Failure is rarely permanently career damaging, provided you actually use the information to improve your approach.

I saw the fear of failure—and the upside of using failure as feedback—play out recently in our company. A facilitator who had been with the firm for a couple of years was scheduled to conduct a program on diversity and inclusion for a financial services client. This individual had worked in the industry for a number of years before joining Global Novations. He was progressing well in his mastery of the material; he was skillful in leading group discussions. Although this was the first time we had conducted a program for this division, Global Novations had a solid reputation in other parts of the company and thought it was a good stretch opportunity for this facilitator.

As it turned out, the class was a very challenging one. In the evaluations, participants commented that they felt the facilitator was "simplistic in his approach to diversity and uninformed about the challenges of their business." Clearly, this was tough feedback. When we met to debrief, the facilitator informed me that he had prepared his letter of resignation. He'd decided he was too young and inexperienced to talk to managers in corporate environments and was thinking about going back to school to get an MBA to make him more credible. All this from one program that didn't go well.

As we talked, he realized that he had been concerned about this program because it was a new division and worried that he didn't know enough. Yet he had studied the facilitator's guide for hours. He had read about the company on the website. He had talked to other facilitators. Certainly, his difficulty wasn't due to a lack of preparation. However, when he received pushback from the group, his anxiety caused him to focus on leading the group to the "right answer" in the facilitator's guide. What he was afraid to do was to stop and listen to the group—and trust that he had enough ability as a facilitator to lead them through a meaningful experience.

Our discussion helped him see that the gap between where he was in his development and where he needed to be wasn't as big as he had imagined. He would have to change the nature of his effort when he got tough questions from the group. Instead of trying to recall the script in the facilitator's guide, he would have to really listen to the challenges the group was facing and help them find their own solutions. Once he understood what he needed to do differently, he was fairly confident he could follow through. Because we had a good relationship with the client, we were able to send the facilitator back to do another program, and he had a much-improved outcome.

Explaining your failure and difficulty in terms of the nature of your effort is absolutely critical. There are three simple questions you can ask yourself to maximize the learning value of any experience: *What* happened? *Why* did it happen? And *how* can I improve? (See Figure 4-3.)

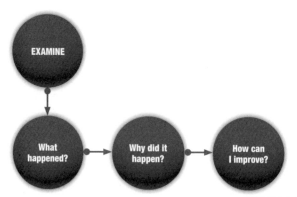

FIGURE 4-3: Using Difficulty as Feedback

What Happened?

You need to be clear about the impact of your work if you are going to make it better moving forward. Too often, we answer this question too broadly—"I messed up"—rather than really understanding specifically what went well and what needs to be done more effectively. For example, if you're looking for a new job and not receiving offers, identify the ineffective aspect of the search process. Are you regularly called for in-person interviews after a phone screening? Are you called back for a second interview? Understanding the specific outcomes helps you make informed decisions about how to focus your effort in ways that are most likely to improve your effectiveness. If your resume isn't getting attention, you probably need to change it or network more strategically. If you're not getting called back, your resume is probably fine, but you might need to improve your interviewing skills.

Why Did It Happen?

When you understand your current outcomes, you have to consider *why* you received them. Answering this question is a critical step. For example, if your recommendation for a product idea isn't accepted, knowing why enables you to be more effective the next time you have an idea to propose. Should you have done a better job of presenting the benefits of the idea? Were there negative consequences for some of the stakeholders that you hadn't anticipated? Did others fail to support you because you hadn't given them enough time to consider your suggestion?

How Can I Improve?

Answering the "why" question paves the way for answering the next question, How can I improve? This answer is the foundation of a strategy for improvement. It will direct your attention toward the steps you need to take. It will lead you to take advantage of your strengths rather than focusing on your weaknesses. It will draw you to resources that you can rely on. Best of all, it allows you to have some degree of certainty that your changed approach will be more successful.

These three questions—What happened? Why did it happen? How can I improve?—focus your attention on the feedback provided by the experience. They facilitate a thought process that builds confidence and zeros in on the effort that will accelerate growth and development.

A NETWORK OF SUPPORT

The second factor that's critical for building confidence is the support of those around you. We all can have good intentions about consistently carrying on an internal dialogue that supports our confidence. However, especially in times of challenge and self-doubt, it's hard to be completely self-sustaining or objective; we all need a network of people who feed our confidence. Although few individuals would dispute the advice to surround themselves with people who support their growth and development, many of us don't actually do it—at least not to the degree we could. How often do we hang out with friends and complain about our bosses or companies? How often do we reinforce one another's feelings that we've been treated unfairly or denied opportunities we deserve?

I'm not saying you shouldn't have a few close friends with whom you can blow off steam, but if listening to you vent is all your friends and colleagues do, you're missing something important. You need a support network that focuses on problem resolution, provides direct and constructive feedback, and gives you access to a wide variety of perspectives and resources. This is the kind of network that can help you build confidence and gain a sense of control over your career.

Problem Resolution

A genuine network of support is one that stretches you and builds your belief that you can improve and accomplish your goals. It includes individuals who help you focus on what you can do to overcome the inevitable challenges of maintaining a meaningful career. A genuine support network doesn't only offer empathy for your frustrations, it helps solve problems. One of the most effective support networks I've been blessed with during my career was a group of professionals I met in the Efficacy seminar I attended thirty years ago. We all listened to one another and were actively supportive, but when one of us had a challenge, the question most often asked was, "So what are you going to do differently?" We never allowed someone to get stuck in blaming external forces. We emphasized personal responsibility as our standard approach to the issues we faced.

We need supportive folks who will help us channel our energy toward effective effort. Find the people who believe in you and can help you build your belief in yourself. Connect with those who will listen to your anger or frustration or confusion without judgment and then push you to be intentional about taking steps to improve your situation. People who support you to meet and overcome a challenge will build your confidence much more quickly than folks who offer sympathy but no support for action.

Direct and Constructive Feedback

Don't limit yourself to a group of unconditional cheerleaders. Too many people make the mistake of cutting out or avoiding those who give them direct feedback about where they need to improve. Friends and colleagues who tell you the truth about an area that needs development are as important to your growth as the individuals who buoy you up in tough times. Real feedback is the best gift you can receive. Seek it out on a regular basis so that you truly understand what you can do to expand your effectiveness.

Many professionals say they want feedback, but their actions send a different message.

I often hear professionals complain that they don't receive good feedback from others. I admit that not enough managers—or colleagues—are skilled in conveying information that helps individuals learn and grow. However, I've also observed that many professionals say they want feedback, but their actions send a different message. Think about your approach. Do you ask for feedback in a way that conveys genuine interest? Do you look for an evaluation that's more specific than "you did a good job"? Are you open to hearing about things you could have done better? Are you willing to listen to a perspective that might be different from your own? Do you refrain from being defensive or argumentative when someone offers an opinion about why you're not achieving the outcomes you want? Do you use the feedback to change your behavior? If you can say yes to most of these questions, it's likely you will receive feedback that helps you grow and become more confident as you see yourself get better and stronger.

At one point in my career, I was consistently receiving good performance reviews, and from what I could tell, I was on track for a promotion to a management-level position. However, when I was passed over for an opportunity I had assumed would be mine, I decided to find out what I could do to accelerate my advancement. At first, my manager, Cathy, told me not to worry; I just needed a little more "seasoning." I remember thinking I could leave it at that or I could push her to give me the real story. So I asked her, in as open and non-defensive way as I could muster, to be direct with me about anything that would make a difference. I could see her trying to decide whether I could take the feedback. She took a risk and gave me insight into some of the subtle things I was doing that made senior staff question my readiness. Some of it was about my style of communication; some of it was about my dress. None of the feedback related to the formal requirements of the job; it all pertained to the unwritten rules of the organization's culture. She took a chance and gave me the scoop on how I was perceived because of my openness to hearing it. With that information, I was able to be much more effective in helping my own cause—and she became an even bigger supporter because she knew I would act on what she told me.

It's tough for many managers to give this kind of feedback; it's often tougher when the manager and employee don't share a background that provides a base of comfort and trust. However, when you send a strong message that you want direct feedback, and when you're willing to make the person providing the feedback feel safe giving it to you, you make yourself "feedback worthy." In return, you're likely to get invaluable information that will accelerate your growth.

Access to Perspectives and Resources

You need a broad network to ensure you receive the variety of support you'll need over the span of your career. Sometimes you might need information about how to get something done or access to a decision maker. Other times you might need help influencing resource and budget allocations or support when a project doesn't turn out as expected. Still other times you might want assistance securing a stretch opportunity or more visibility. The kinds of support required throughout one's career are numerous. Only a very broad network can provide you with all the support that's necessary.

Knowing how to get access to the counsel and resources you need builds confidence that you can engineer your desired outcomes. We'll talk more about how you do this in Chapter 7, but the first step in receiving the support you require is asking for it. That probably seems pretty straightforward, but how often do you struggle with a problem when there's probably someone who would be glad to coach you? How often are you afraid to ask for a resource or a different kind of assignment? People can't give support if they don't know what you need.

To get support, you also have to give it. When someone needs your help or effort, are you willing to do that extra bit? Do others see you as someone they can rely on? Do you positively affect the tone and productivity of your work group? If you present yourself as someone committed to helping the organization succeed, and as someone who will positively influence the productivity of others, you have something to offer that will make most managers and colleagues willing to offer their support in return.

PROTECT YOUR CONFIDENCE

Some people and situations are more likely to test your confidence than others. It's doubtful that you can avoid those individuals or situations entirely. What you can do, however, is minimize their capacity to undermine your confidence and your effort. Anticipate situations that are likely to erode your confidence and develop a strategy to stay focused on your belief in yourself and your ability to work effectively. If you have a manager whose style undermines your confidence, seek out someone who can coach you about how to develop a more productive relationship. If you have colleagues who cause you to doubt yourself, you might have to be judicious about the time you spend with them. If you have specific kinds of responsibilities that cause you anxiety, you might need to develop strategies to focus yourself and reduce your stress level. Some people I know write down all the things they do well when their confidence is feeling shaky. Others go for a run. Still others write about their feelings in a diary.

If you know you're headed into a particularly tough assignment, arrange for support ahead of time. Who can help you prepare? What helps you to relax? How will you recharge and reenergize? Do you need to arrange some extra time with friends or mentors, or plan a weekend away? Do you need to block out time on your schedule to exercise? I also recommend that after a demanding project, you debrief with someone who will be balanced in reinforcing your strengths and in giving you specific strategies for improving. Each of us is likely to have different approaches that ground us in our most confident and competent selves. Figure out what works for you and be deliberate in protecting your confidence.

Confidence is a fragile thing. And it isn't something you automatically have. Confidence is something you build over time and strategically nurture, especially during times when it is likely to be tried. Be intentional about cultivating the confidence that you need to accomplish what's important to you. The more confident you are, the bigger your reach will be. You will dare to have a broader vision, you will set more challenging goals, and you will create more choice for yourself. You will, in short, be a more developed person.

ADOPT KEY IDEAS

- Attribute your successes to your ability and effort so that each success boosts your confidence.
- Explain your failures in terms of ineffective effort—not lack of ability. This leaves your confidence intact and stimulates more intensive effort.
- Failure is not an indication of your worth; it is feedback about how to get better.
- Build confidence by creating a support network that focuses on problem solving, provides direct and constructive feedback, and gives you access to a broad range of perspectives and resources.

BEGIN NOW

Replace your confidence-eroding self-talk with a dialogue that reinforces your belief in your capability to grow and develop over time.

Think of an area where you tend to cite lack of ability or forces outside your control as reasons for your difficulties. On the next page, in the left-hand column, list examples of the explanations that erode your confidence. In the right-hand column, list alternatives that would be more likely to support your confidence and effective effort.

CONFIDENCE-ERODING SELF-TALK	CONFIDENCE-BUILDING SELF-TALK
Example: *I'll never be good at networking. I'm not an outgoing person.*	*I'm most comfortable talking to people one to one; I need to initiate individual conversations with a greater range of colleagues.*

When you find yourself explaining your difficulties with the self-talk in the left-hand column, consciously reframe the dialogue so as to build your confidence that you can engineer a more desirable outcome.

LEARN MORE

Assess the quality of the support you have available to foster your development by completing the "Support Survey." You can download it from *The Power of Choice* website (www.powerofchoice.net).

MAKE YOUR EFFORT EFFECTIVE

Having confidence is critically important to your development, but it alone is not enough to enable your long-term growth. Confidence has to lead to effective effort because effective effort is what expands your skills and capabilities and drives your career.

One of the most common mistakes professionals make is to confuse working hard with working effectively. Sanjay and Germaine are two examples. Currently a manager in a marketing firm, Sanjay wants to be promoted to a director-level position within the next two years. He therefore spends hours correcting the work of his direct reports. He also participates in almost every one of his team's project meetings to ensure that the right decisions are made, and he gives his direct reports limited authority over day-to-day operations. Sanjay is definitely working hard—sixty hours a week—but he is not working effectively. He is not developing his staff's capabilities, and he spends very little time fostering new client relationships or cultivating sales opportunities, both of which are critical for him to earn additional opportunities in the company. So in spite of his long hours, he is unlikely to receive the promotion he wants.

Effective effort results in your desired outcomes or moves you toward those outcomes.

Germaine wants to be seen as the go-to person in her department. She works at least ten hours a day processing claims for a casualty insurance company. She's been doing the same job for five years, and she's very good at what she does. Her boss asked her to be part of a project team charged with evaluating a new software package, but she declined due to the demands of her workload.

Both Sanjay and Germaine are working hard, but neither is receiving the best return on their investment of time and energy. They're not learning new skills, they're not developing the skills of others, and they're not expanding the ways in which they contribute to their organizations. I assure you that in each of their work groups, there is someone who is putting in the same number of hours (or maybe even fewer) but who is getting better career traction and a higher rate of development because their effort is more effective.

The key indicator that your effort is effective is that it achieves your desired outcomes or it moves you closer to those goals. If you're working hard but not accomplishing what's important to you, start by examining the nature of your effort.

You can make your effort more effective by following these four critical steps: choose what you want as an outcome, focus on what you can control, expand your skills incrementally, and align your goals with your organization's needs. (See Figure 5-1.) If you incorporate these steps into your career strategy, you're more likely to get the best return on the investment of your time and energy.

FIGURE 5-1: Make Your Effort Effective

CHOOSE WHAT YOU WANT AS AN OUTCOME

Effective effort starts with the end in mind. What do you want to accomplish—in the short and the long term? It's hard to be strategic about shaping your career and garnering the support of others if you don't know the outcomes you're trying to achieve. What do you want to complete by the end of the day or the end of the year? What do you want people thinking or doing at the end of a meeting? If you don't like your current work situation, what will make it better? If you're frustrated with a colleague, how do you want to change the nature of the relationship? The more precisely you can identify a goal, the more likely you will be able to figure out a strategy for accomplishing it.

This might seem obvious, but I'm struck by how often individuals are unclear about the outcomes they want. Imagine that you're driving and you don't know where you want to go. Without that orientation toward a final destination, it's easy to spend a lot of time going around in circles. It's also more likely you'll get distracted by the obstacles in your path. When you know your destination, however, you can choose some interesting detours, but you're still likely to make it to where you want to go. A clear vision keeps you focused on the effective effort that enables you to accomplish your goal.

When I started working on this book, I didn't have a dedicated time or consistent process for writing, and I wasn't making much progress. I finally realized that if I was going to get this book published, I had to structure my work life to support the effort. I also realized that I needed a team that could help me manage the many aspects of editing and producing a book. Clarity about my desired outcome—publishing the book—helped direct my attention to what it would take to make it happen.

Just as it's important to know where you're headed short-term, it's also critical to identify what you want from your career long-term. What will give you satisfaction and a sense of achievement in the long run? You don't necessarily need to identify a particular position or type of job that you ultimately want, but you do need to give some thought to how you want to invest your time and energy. What motivates or interests you? What makes you enjoy coming to work? What impact do you want to have? What values are most important to you? How would you like to honor those values in the work you do? If you pay attention to what engages you and what doesn't and then craft your work as best you can to align with those interests, you are much more likely to feel fulfilled in your career.

Some professionals are clear about their interests and career goals early on. However, for many of us, it takes some trial and error to determine where we're motivated to invest significant time and effort.

My own career journey is a good example. When I was growing up, I always said I wanted to be a doctor. But after my freshman year in college, I had to be honest with myself: I wasn't motivated to pursue the years of academic training that becoming a doctor required. Still, I wanted to make a good living, have the opportunity to use my people skills, and exert influence in an organization. Business seemed to be a field that would fulfill those aspirations, so I changed my major to cost accounting. After my junior year, I landed a summer internship as an accountant and made significant money—at least when compared with my past summer jobs in an ice cream store. Unfortunately, the experience showed me that accounting wasn't for me. I wanted a career that had more to do with people than with balance sheets.

It was now the beginning of my senior year, and I desperately needed to figure out my career direction. I solicited the help of a career counselor at my college. At her suggestion, I switched to human resources. Fortunately, I loved it! I had to stay an extra semester to complete the requirements, but I appreciated every aspect of the HR field I studied during my last year and a half, and my good grades were proof of my interest in the field.

When I landed my first job, it was in HR in the retail industry, and I stayed in that field for a number of years. My relationship skills were well-utilized, but after some time, I realized I wasn't fulfilling my salary goals or those I had for strategic influence. To generate more income and to work in a position with profit-and-loss responsibility, I took on a role as a store manager. The switch into the operations area of the business led to several more promotions and prepared me to eventually become an officer in the company.

Measured in terms of influence and money, I had done of good job of accomplishing my vision when I became an officer, but I wasn't fulfilled. When I asked myself why, I realized that over the course of my career, I had come to truly value helping others develop, and I wanted to work in an industry where people were the central part of the mission. Going to work for the company that is now Global Novations was a way to bring all the threads together. I could do what I had learned I liked best—coach and mentor, build business relationships, negotiate deals, steer the outcomes of a team—and make enough money to support my family while doing it.

By continuing to ask myself, "What do I want as an outcome?" I was able to navigate through the twists and turns of my career in a way that kept me coming back to the things that were most important to me. Keeping my vision in front of me also helped me decline opportunities that weren't in line with what I wanted long-term. For instance, at one point, I was offered a promotion within the human resources department. Since I had figured out I needed a store manager job to meet my goals for influence within the organization, I said no to that opportunity without having second thoughts.

What pattern do you see in your own life? Look carefully at how you choose to spend your time and at the work that proves most satisfying and energizing. You get a big payoff when you invest effort in something you care about. You come to work gladly. You're naturally drawn to improving. And you are willing to work through the problems that arise. Knowing what's important to you provides clarity when you have to make critical decisions about which opportunities you will pursue and which you will forego.

Regardless of the outcomes you choose, you also have to be willing to accept the consequences of your choices as there are likely to be some trade-offs. If you choose a high-powered career that requires extensive travel, you are likely to miss out on some family milestones. If you choose to work independently, you're likely to miss out on some level of collegial support. If you choose to invest the majority of your discretionary energy in your personal life rather than your career, there is likely to be an impact on your perceived value to your organization.

Take the time to identify what's most important to you. Then be willing to accept the consequences of your choices.

I'm not suggesting you fear the consequences or avoid pursuing the outcomes that are important to you. Rather, I'm proposing that you take the time to identify what's most important to you—and what you could give up. Fully consider the likely consequences of your choices and then accept or actively manage them rather than be surprised by or resentful of them. Being clear about your desired outcomes and the consequences increases the likelihood that the investment of your effort will give you a return that you value.

FOCUS ON WHAT YOU CAN CONTROL

Effective effort is focused on what you can control. Remember, a key principle of Efficacy is, *It's not the stimulus, it's the response.* You can't change the personality of your boss, but you can choose how the two of you interact. You can't keep the economy from taking a nose dive, but you can control how you respond to the challenges of a tight business climate.

Focus your effort on outcomes that are challenging but, at the same time, realistic. In other words, don't settle for the status quo. Look for outcomes that require you to stretch yourself. Try to improve a situation or learn something new, but concentrate on short-term goals that you have a reasonable likelihood of accomplishing. It's difficult to work effectively if you're fixated on achieving something that's currently unrealistic. If the gap between your current skill level and the demands of a situation is too great, you'll be frustrated, and it won't provide you with the feedback you need to improve. It's better to direct your energy toward goals that stretch you and build upon the foundation you have in place.

When I lift the hood of my car, I can't interpret the significance of the squeaks and knocking sounds I hear. I would need to start with a basic repair course if I wanted to learn to fix my own car. A mechanic, on the other hand, can listen for a few minutes and predict the problem with a fair degree of accuracy. The sounds he hears can guide his effective effort because his current level of proficiency allows him to better understand the problem.

Too often, I've seen professionals persist in using an approach even though it is not producing the outcome they desire—a sure sign that their current goal is unrealistic or that they need to develop some additional expertise. They don't pay attention to the feedback that's telling them that their approach isn't working. They refuse to cross what I call the "line of respectability." They hesitate to seek coaching because they are afraid to disclose their deficiency. Or they are reluctant to make a lateral move even though it might fill a skill gap. They won't ask for help from a colleague or direct report. They would rather continue to struggle than acknowledge their current level of development and devise a more effective strategy to improve. Unfortunately, their growth often stalls.

A colleague once recounted the approach she took in her first college economics course. It impressed me as a good example of paying attention to feedback and focusing on what you can control in order to accelerate your development. The course textbook was dense; the lecturer was dry. She eked by with a C on her first test. She tried to spend more hours studying but was frustrated and overwhelmed by the content. Finally, she said to herself, "There's got to be something I can do to get a better grade." She went to the local library and ended up in the children's section reading books about how the financial system works. Those books introduced her to the basics of economics. Once she was more grounded in the topic, she found the college textbook more understandable, and she was able to take better advantage of her study group's support. She ended the term with a B+. Her willingness to accept her initial level of development in the subject and read children's books to bring herself up to speed always impressed me. She took control of her situation to engineer better results.

When you're feeling overwhelmed or out of control, break down your goals into more manageable chunks. Seek support and coaching. Consider whether another approach might be more effective. Remember, effective effort either accomplishes your desired outcomes or moves you closer to your goal. If you're not getting the results you want, you need to face that fact. Don't blame others; don't give up. Focus on the steps you can take to achieve at least a small success. What can you control or influence? Even a small accomplishment creates momentum that moves you toward your ultimate vision.

EXPAND YOUR SKILLS INCREMENTALLY

When I advise you to focus on the things you can control, I'm not suggesting that you limit your goals. Quite the contrary. Dream big; have a grand vision for yourself. Dare to imagine that you can accomplish great things.

However, you have to work toward your vision *incrementally*. Development is a process of continuously stretching yourself. Start with what's possible and important to accomplish today. When you reach your first goal, take on a little more challenge. When you're successful at this next level, stretch a bit more. Over time, after a series of successes and probably some setbacks, a goal that was once unrealistic becomes attainable. (See Figure 5-2.) Through an incremental process of development, you expand the scope of possibilities.

FIGURE 5-2: Expand Your Skills Incrementally

I often have conversations with sales professionals inside and outside our company about "unrealistic" annual sales goals. I always challenge these individuals to begin by focusing their effort on a quarterly sales number they think is a reasonable stretch—regardless of the ultimate target. When their attention is on a goal that feels possible rather than on one they fear is impossible, they typically reach the realistic, but still challenging, goal they set for themselves. This initial good result helps them learn which sales approaches are effective and which aren't so they build their expertise and increase their confidence.

Then I encourage them to stretch a bit more: what additional revenue might be possible? More often than not, by pursuing their sales targets in incremental stages, they meet the original "unrealistic" goal. And if they don't, we both have more accurate information to set a challenging but realistic target for the following year.

When you're confronted with expectations that seem unrealistic, focus on a challenging but realistic goal. As you experience success, stretch yourself and take on something more challenging. This incremental process of development will enable you to accomplish many goals that were originally unrealistic and out of your control.

Sometimes individuals limit their development because they are afraid to take risks outside the bounds of what they are sure they can accomplish. It can appear "safe" to limit yourself to areas where you've had a history of success and avoid stretching yourself to develop new expertise, but playing it safe is actually a pretty risky strategy. Job requirements change. The competitive environment changes. The company's expectations of you change. If you don't stretch your capabilities over time, you minimize your options. Proactively pursuing incremental learning and development gives you opportunities; it expands your circle of control.

That said, sometimes people jump too far too fast. There's no great harm in over-stretching. In fact, if you don't overreach from time to time, it's probably a sign you're playing it too safe. The harm comes if you don't adjust your approach when you get the feedback that your strategy is unrealistic, given your current skill set or the demands of the external circumstances.

The diversity officer for a global company called us in recently to help her with her strategy. It was her first year on the job, and she had come to it full of ambition and great ideas. She had planned to host a global conference, start an aggressive recruiting strategy to boost the number of women worldwide in the company, and establish mentoring teams to support these women's development. Now, six months later, she was

totally burned out from working nights
and weekends, and she was angry with
her boss for not giving her more
support.

> If you don't pair your talents and work with your organization's needs, you are not likely to be rewarded for your effort.

As we talked about her budget
and staff resources, I learned that
she had only a part-time assistant
and a budget of $40,000. No won-
der she was exasperated! Her vision
was a wonderful one, but it was unrealistic given the current size of her budget and
staff and the amount of executive support. Together we crafted a plan
that was more incremental. This year she would host a U.S.-based conference, not a global one. She would focus on networking with the heads of
business units to build their understanding of the connections between
diversity and inclusion and the organization's goals. She would work on
creating a more effective working relationship with her manager. When
the diversity officer focused on plans she felt she could accomplish, she
felt much less frustrated and burned out. In addition, these challenging
but realistic goals gave her a better chance of getting buy-in for a bigger
budget and more staff for the next fiscal year.

When you find yourself losing momentum or becoming overwhelmed, identify the steps you can take that will ensure some incremental progress. The strategy of expanding your skills over time keeps your
focus on what you can control, and it builds your confidence that you can
be successful in the long run.

ALIGN YOUR GOALS WITH YOUR ORGANIZATION'S NEEDS

When professionals are deciding how to invest their efforts, I find they
often underestimate the importance of aligning their efforts with the

needs of the organization. You can be talented and busy with many responsibilities, but if you don't pair your talents and work with the organization's needs, you are not likely to be rewarded for your effort—or given opportunities to develop further.

Start by aligning your efforts with the goals of your manager and others you support. You are much more likely to receive both recognition for your value and opportunities to grow if the people you work with most closely see you as someone they can rely on to accomplish what's important to them. What are they charged with? What makes them successful? What activities are particularly important because of their goals and objectives?

Every manager and organization is looking for employees who can expand *how* they contribute. Early on, the expectation is that you learn to do your job well; you develop your own ideas and judgment, rather than continuing to depend on others for day-to-day guidance. The organization also expects you to make connections with others that enable you to get things done efficiently. Do you know whom to go to for information and support? Have you established connections such that others are willing to work collaboratively with you?

Once you've learned to do your job well, your organization looks to you to influence others' work. Because you have developed deep technical expertise, your organization rightly expects you to coach and mentor team members and junior employees, either as a colleague or a manager. You are expected to contribute your ideas for improving work processes and outcomes. By this point you are not only contributing the value of your own work but also magnifying your contribution through your impact on others. This is where both Sanjay and Germaine were falling short. They were doing excellent work themselves, but they weren't delivering higher-order results by expanding their impact on the work of those around them.

Keep in mind this need to grow your capacity to contribute through others, and be alert to the talents, skills, and behaviors expected of high performers in your current position. Pay attention to the competencies required for promotion or additional opportunities. After you've determined the skills and behaviors that are important to your organization, you'll be able to make a conscious choice. Are these talents and skills important to you? Are you willing to learn what's required? If not, it's unlikely you'll be motivated to invest the effort to become a high performer in this job. Take responsibility to find a better fit for your talents and interests.

Although every professional has to adapt to the requirements of the organization, I find that in most organizations there's more room for negotiation and flexibility than you might assume, *if you have already established yourself as a valuable contributor and you position your needs in terms of benefits to the organization.* Be willing to test the limits of the organization's culture to accommodate your unique talents, interests, and values. Is it really required to work from "eight to faint" to get ahead? Is there more room for different points of view than might be apparent on the surface? Professionals are often surprised by the latitude they have when they are willing to invest in creating an honest partnership with the organization and the individuals they work with every day.

In 2010, like many companies, Global Novations was working hard to operate profitably in a challenging economic environment. We asked our facilitators to take on heavy workloads, which often required them to be on the road for several weeks in a row. Understandably, this resulted in some tension with personal travel preferences and family needs.

One of our facilitators took a very effective approach to solving her dilemma. Wanting to limit her travel, she aggressively researched options in the company that might fit her skills. She discovered that we were expanding our webinar offerings in response to clients' requests to reduce the expenses of face-to-face training. She studied webinar design on her own time and offered herself as a resource to design and train virtually. Although she still had to travel some, she could supplement client engagements that required being on the road with the design and delivery of webinars, which she could do from the office. She developed a new expertise; we grew our webinar business. Most important for her, she was able to make a meaningful contribution without getting on a plane every week.

This facilitator's family needs were legitimate, but her approach was effective because she focused her solution on a need of the organization rather than leading with her own interests. Such an approach might not always work out perfectly, and it certainly won't fall into your lap. However, the more you can align your interests with the needs of the organization, the more likely you are to be highly engaged in and committed to your work—and to win your organization's support.

THE HIGHEST RETURN ON INVESTMENT OF YOUR TIME AND EFFORT

However you define it, success requires you to choose how you will invest your effort. When you make these choices wisely, based on an understanding of your desired outcomes and the organization's needs, you increase the impact of your effort. Know what you want as outcome, focus on what you can control, expand your skills incrementally to move toward your vision, and align yourself with the organization's needs. These four principles won't guarantee success every time, but managing your career with them in mind creates momentum toward accomplishing your vision and maximizes your return on the investment of your effort.

ADOPT KEY IDEAS

- Choose what you want as an outcome—and accept the consequences of your choice.
- Focus on what you can control.
- Expand your skills incrementally to move toward your vision.
- Align yourself with the organization's needs.

BEGIN NOW

Identify an area where you would like to devote more effective effort in order to reach a desired outcome.

- What outcome do you want from your effort?
- How does your desired outcome benefit your organization?
- What are you doing now that is moving you toward that outcome?
- What are you doing that is impeding your momentum? What do you need to do differently?
- What action steps will you take to make your effort more effective and move you closer to your goal?

LEARN MORE

Take the Career Orientations Self-Assessment, which covers the five factors that influence career decisions: challenge, balance, security, advancement, and freedom. You'll learn more about how these factors influence your career outcomes. You can download it from *The Power of Choice* website (www.powerofchoice.net).

LEVERAGE
RELATIONAL SKILLS

You can have focused effort, but you won't be valued as an integral part of your organization unless leaders and colleagues know who you are and are comfortable working with you. Teamwork, client service, information sharing, problem solving—all these activities require individuals to interact with one another productively and with as little friction as possible. Given the importance of these interpersonal activities in today's workplaces, people who have developed relational skills, who have the social grace to navigate a broad spectrum of interactions and create comfortable and trusting relationships, are the most sought after by leaders and coworkers. It's only through exposure and connections that others know to call upon you for your expertise. It's only through relationships that you learn whose influence and support can help you to accomplish an objective. And most important, relational skills enable you to work with others for mutual gains.

Relationships don't happen automatically. First you have to put effort into making the connections. How much effort do you currently expend on creating relationships? Do folks inside and outside your organization know who you are and what you have to offer? Do you have people you can rely on for support and advice? How good are your relationships with coworkers you interact with every day? Would they say you're someone they can count on?

The guidelines in this chapter will enable you to be more strategic and intentional in how you expand the breadth and depth of your relationships.

TAKE ADVANTAGE OF OPPORTUNITIES TO CONNECT WITH OTHERS

Relationships all start with getting to know others—and helping them get to know you. They begin with the simple gesture of introducing yourself.

I'm amazed at how often professionals squander important opportunities to make connections with others. Recently, I gave a talk at a company-sponsored networking event for the African-American Employee Resource Group. I was pleased to see that the event was structured so that I would speak for about thirty minutes, the president of the company would join us for a meet-and-greet reception, and we would then reconvene for a question-and-answer period. During my talk, I directed my remarks toward the development of relational and influence skills, so I expected the group was well-primed to take advantage of this wonderful opportunity to introduce themselves to their chief executive.

I was fascinated to watch what happened. The president who came expressly to network with this group started up a conversation with me. We stood in the middle of the room in a very accessible location, but *none of the attendees* came up to introduce themselves. Granted, the president could have reached out to the employees, but certainly anyone in this group could have walked up to him and initiated a conversation.

When we got back together for the Q&A, I asked the group why no one took advantage of the opportunity to meet the president. Some employees said that it felt awkward to interrupt; others commented that they wouldn't know what to say; still others weren't sure the president would be interested in meeting them.

All those reservations are understandable, but letting their discomfort drive their actions meant they lost an invaluable opportunity—in fact, one that had been specifically set up for networking. How often do you forego such important opportunities? How could you take better advantage of them to connect with people, and how would making these connections benefit your career?

For many professionals, initiating a conversation is the primary stumbling block. In advance, prepare an introduction of yourself that conveys the essence of what you have to offer—your job, career interests, or personal attributes. Try to make it memorable. One of our consultants recently worked with a young Asian manager at a top U.S. consulting firm. The manager was a quiet, unassuming guy who wanted to figure out a way to convey a lasting impression. As they were working together, he mentioned that he spent his weekends racing motorcycles. The image of him in leathers wearing a full-face helmet and dragging his knee on the ground to make sharp turns certainly would help others remember him. When he added that he brought to his work the same passion for challenge and calculated risk-taking that made him an effective motorcycle racer, he had all the necessary pieces to create a great introduction for himself.

No matter their position in an organization, people want to meet interesting people. With a little upfront preparation to put your best foot forward, you can take advantage of these opportunities.

LOOK FOR COMMON GROUND

A relationship, of course, is much more than being acquainted. It is an association that builds gradually when people spend time together and get to know one another. Look for common ground that will serve as the basis for relationships. What are leaders and colleagues responsible for accomplishing? What are their goals? Be genuinely interested in learning their story. Reserve judgment on the differences you encounter. Rather than focusing on reasons to avoid or distrust others, be curious and look for ways to connect.

Understand that common ground comes in many different forms. You don't have to share a person's gender or cultural identity to have something in common. You do have to share enough about who you are and the expertise you bring to the table to uncover the similarities that build familiarity and comfort with one another.

Sharing information about oneself can be uncomfortable for people who feel different from the majority of those in their work group. If you are concerned about how you will be judged and awarded opportunities in the organization, self-disclosure can seem like a big leap of faith. Why risk giving those around you a reason to reject or discount you by revealing more than the basics about yourself? Our cultural norms might discourage us from sharing personal information outside our trusted circle of family and friends; we might have learned that it's inappropriate to voice personal opinions to others, especially those in authority.

A colleague recently facilitated a dialogue between a group of white and black women. After some significant time spent building openness and trust among members of the group, the conversation turned to cultural patterns the women observed about their black or white colleagues. The white women commented that the black women were standoffish and closed. The black women thought the white women were too nosy. Clearly, there were different cultural rules at play that influenced how much disclosure was important for building a meaningful relationship. Neither group is right or wrong in their preferred style. However, the judgments about the other group were getting in the way of finding common ground to build a connection.

Those of us from backgrounds that are different from the majority of our coworkers have to step out of our comfort zones in order to increase the quality of our relationships. The deepest connections tend to form when we share our authentic selves, including our interests, opinions, and vulnerabilities. I'm not advocating that you share all the details of your personal life or divulge your innermost fears. However, you do have to be deliberate about creating a basis for connection. Leaders and peers don't connect with a title or set of accomplishments—they connect with a person.

> Leaders and peers don't connect with a title or a set of accomplishments—they connect with a person.

I recently met Eduardo, a young Mexican-American. He grew up in Texas in a tight-knit community and had deep connections to his extended family and friends. He was the first in his family to go to college and was delighted when he landed a job as a production manager at a consumer-products plant where he'd interned during college. After three years, he was offered a transfer and promotion to a facility in Ohio that he accepted gladly (although with a little trepidation about leaving the area where he'd grown up). Now six months into the new job, he has found coworkers to be polite but reserved. He feels that his team doesn't really trust him. He and his family get few social invitations, and on the few occasions they've been invited to someone's home for dinner or a social gathering, Eduardo feels others avoid him and make little effort to engage him in conversation. He's painfully aware that his family is the only Hispanic one in his neighborhood, and one of only a few at the local school. Eduardo misses Texas and his old job. He wonders whether he's made a mistake.

When you're adjusting to the demands of a new job and working with colleagues who have backgrounds different from your own, it can be especially difficult to reach out to them. As we talked, Eduardo admitted that he's been focused on the operational aspects of his new job and not on getting to know people. His own discomfort with the new community, both at work and at home, have caused him to pull back from interacting with others. To turn the situation around, he has to realize he can't wait for coworkers to reach out to him; he has to take the initiative. He also has to acknowledge it's a process that takes time. The shared ties of community and family jump-started his relationships when he was in Texas. In his new community, there won't instantly be the same level of connection, but he has to make the effort and start somewhere.

How Eduardo might begin really depends on his style. He could dedicate a half hour every morning to walking around the plant and checking in with folks—personally and professionally. The more he does this, the more he will learn about his coworkers and their interests, and the more they will learn about him. Or he could eat lunch with different groups every day. He could also schedule some after-work social gatherings.

When you become proactive about building other people's comfort with you, you are much more likely to find common ground that will serve as the basis for strong relationships regardless of differences in your cultures or backgrounds.

TRUST IS AN OUTCOME, NOT A REQUIREMENT

I often hear, "I could never have a relationship with him; he can't be trusted." Certainly trust is important in a relationship. Everyone wants to know that others will work on their behalf, won't jeopardize their interests, and will be predictable in their actions. However, it's a mistake to believe that trust comes automatically. It's also a mistake to believe that someone who has shown to be untrustworthy in one relationship is *necessarily* untrustworthy in *all* relationships.

You have much more control over establishing the basis for good working relationships than you realize. You can't guarantee that people will work on your behalf or support you in all instances. However, by following these four steps, you can shape your relationships in a manner that improves the odds of a mutually beneficial connection (see Figure 6-1):

- *Determine shared objectives.* Sometimes, we focus too much on ourselves and what we want out of a situation and give too little thought and attention to the incentive for others to support our interests. To unearth shared interests that can serve as a basis for partnership, you have to listen. You have to be genuinely interested in other people's points of view. If you see others only as obstacles to be managed or overcome, you are less likely to find a basis for mutual support or willing collaboration. If you see others only as a tool for your own interests, they are likely to see through your manipulation.

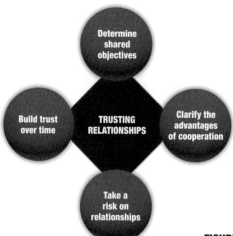

FIGURE 6-1: How to Build Trusting Relationships

- *Clarify the advantages of cooperation.* The shared objectives might be clear to you, but sometimes you have to help others see what they can gain from working together. Paint a picture of the benefits for them.
- *Take a risk on relationships.* There's no guarantee that others will always keep their end of the bargain. However, I believe most people are capable of—even prefer to have—honest, fair, and reciprocal relationships.

Many of us are skeptical that individuals "not like us" can become good working partners. The suspicion that "those people"—whether they're white guys or senior managers or staff from another department—will always "protect their own" gets in the way of seeking a way to have mutually supportive relationships. If you are willing to step out of your comfort zone to build trust and show you can be depended on to support their interests, it increases the likelihood that the other party will do so as well.

- *Build trust over time.* Trust comes from a series of successes in a working relationship. Don't bet your most important goal on the sole support of someone with whom you haven't yet developed a good working relationship. Each of you needs to understand the benefits of your collaboration and the cost if you fail to support one another. Start small and risk more in the relationship as each of you learns what's important to the other and how you can work together most effectively.

Early in my career, a store manager named George was assigned to be the human resources manager—and my boss—at my Detroit store location. George considered this position to be a demotion, since he was being moved out of the suburban store he'd worked at previously. He was a white man with a gruff personality. He made disparaging remarks about the customers we served, and he was openly critical of staff, especially the intellectual capacity of blacks, including me. My colleagues advised me that under George my career would be toast and to get out quickly. However, George had to sign off on any transfer or promotion I was offered—and I wasn't ready to let him drive me out of the company.

I decided that I would focus on finding ways within my job responsibilities to support George's priorities and make him look good within the company. In partnership with many employees at the store, I worked to boost our customer service scores and reduce our inventory shortage. These improvements gave our store—and George—lots of positive visibility. As a result, his negative energy toward me began to lessen, and we were able to develop a useful and productive working relationship.

I never came to like the man. However, by establishing a relationship with him rather than seeing him as an obstacle to my goals, I gained the chance to move on to a bigger role with more responsibility at another store. I concentrated on finding the common ground we had—we both needed the store to be successful—and putting my effort into outcomes that would benefit us both.

For the cause of the relationship, I initially ignored some of his rude behavior and condescending comments about me and my colleagues. As we got to know one another better, we established a relationship where I could call him on the behavior I found most offensive. I never would have had this leverage with him if I hadn't invested in the relationship.

Some would call this manipulative; others might say I sold out. Each of us has to choose where we draw the line of integrity. From my point of view, I wasn't damaging George or myself in any way (the ethical line for me). I was managing the situation so that I could maintain momentum in accomplishing what was important to me rather than let someone else dictate my future.

PROFESSIONAL RELATIONSHIPS ARE NOT FRIENDSHIPS

You can choose which relationships you invest in and which ones you don't, but understand that for the sake of your goals, you will sometimes have to invest in relationships you don't particularly enjoy or that you initially find uncomfortable. As important as it is to build trusting professional relationships, they are not friendships. Relationships at work might evolve into friendships, but that's not a requirement. Rather, professional relationships are about connecting with someone to accomplish mutually important outcomes. You might not like someone else's style or how they choose to spend their time outside of work. They might not particularly like you. However, such factors are not sufficient to write off the possibility of establishing a productive relationship. If you start by assuming the other person is too irritating, too untrustworthy, or too closed-minded to ever have a relationship with, you will never figure out a way to work together. In fact, you're not likely to put much effort into the relationship at all.

Few of us question the importance of being intentional about delivering quality work or meeting performance objectives. Relational skills are every bit as essential to your career success as the quality of your output. So why not pay the same attention to developing in this area as you do in your area of technical expertise? The more flexible and strategic you are in connecting with a wide variety of individuals at all levels inside and outside the organization, the greater your options for leveraging the support and resources of others to get things done.

DEVELOP A CONNECTION WITH YOUR MANAGER

Just as I had to find a way to work with George, you must always develop a relationship with your manager. It doesn't matter if he or she is remote, uninvolved, harsh, abrupt, or incompetent. Your manager is typically the person who has the most influence on the opportunities you receive, so you'll get better support and be able to create more options for yourself if you maintain a good relationship.

Your manager has to trust that you are an individual who will represent him or her well through the quality of your work and through your presentation of the team to others. No manager wants to feel that someone on the team doesn't really care about the work or, even worse, is working at cross purposes.

If you don't know what's important to your manager, *ask*. Most managers are glad to discuss their goals for the group. They might even be willing to share where they'd like to go in their careers. Any manager will be heartened to hear you're on board with his or her objectives.

If you don't understand your manager's work style, ask how he or she wants to interact with you and what he or she needs to work effectively with you. For example, is your manager a person who loves to talk through all the angles of a problem or someone who wants only the bottom line? Does he or she want to know the details of your projects or only the problems you are experiencing? The better you understand your manager's expectations of you in terms of deliverables and working style, the better you'll be able to shape an effective working relationship.

BE STRATEGIC IN BUILDING PERSONAL CONNECTIONS

Building relationships isn't about the number of connections you have on LinkedIn or how many friends you have on Facebook. It's about securing the connections that grow your social capital—your ability to exchange knowledge, guide the flow of information, secure resources, and in general tap into a reserve of cooperation, problem solving, and creativity. As you plan how you will connect with others, consider the four characteristics of an effective network (see Figure 6-2):

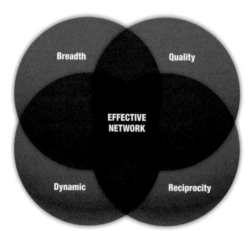

FIGURE 6-2: The Characteristics of an Effective Network

- *Breadth.* Do you have connections at many levels, inside and outside your current organization? You will always need information about the priorities in other parts of your company and access to the influencers. You'll need to stay abreast of the trends and thought leaders in your industry. Get to know as many people as you can at as many levels as you can.

That said, don't be so focused on getting to know your company and industry leaders that you forget your peers or those who report to you. Colleagues and subordinates are more willing to offer their ideas and their effort if they have a relationship with you and are invested in your success. You need to know everyone who can help solve a problem, give you a perspective you don't have, or connect you to a resource.

Consider whether your network gives you access to a wide variety of perspectives and experience. If everyone in your network shares your background, socioeconomic status, and politics, you're likely to be missing valuable input. Do you eat lunch with the same folks every day? Do you socialize only with individuals like yourself? Do you involve yourself in outside activities attended by the same kinds of people you work with? If the answer is yes, strongly consider expanding the breadth of your network.

- *Quality.* Too often, we stop at breadth when we think of networking. "I know a lot of people, so I'm all set." However, when you're focused on relationships, not just networking, you'll want to evaluate the quality of your connections. Have you spent enough time with them so that there's a true understanding of their value? Is there mutual respect? Are the professionals you're connected with able and willing to use their influence on your behalf? Can you count on them for support or information when you need it? No matter how many people you know, if the quality of the relationships isn't strong enough that they will work on your behalf, it doesn't matter how big your contact list is.

- *Reciprocity.* The quality of your network is often linked to the reciprocal nature of your connections. If you get something from others, they expect something in return. Some might want the satisfaction of watching young talent grow or support to sell an idea. Others might need your resources, your advice, your effort, or your access to someone else. You can be a role model, sounding board, an advocate, or a coach. You don't have to know specifically how you will be of service to others or how they will be of service to you in order to start a relationship. In fact, the whole purpose of making connections is to learn about others and figure out the resources and support you might have to offer each other.

  If you find yourself hesitant to make connections, maybe it's because you haven't identified your value in your own mind. Professionals who don't know their value are less likely to reach out. Why should people get to know you? What strengths do you bring? Being clear about your value makes it easier to be a giver, not just a receiver; owning your value gives you capital for building a meaningful network of connections.

- *Dynamic.* Your relationships will change over time. Your career priorities and development needs will change. You will have to add to your network or invest differently in some relationships over the course of your career. For example, early on you need to establish a broad network of connections inside your organization so that you learn how to get things done in the context of your responsibilities. As your career progresses, you typically need broader outside connections to stay current with the trends in your industry and relevant to the evolving needs of your clients or customers.

  Too many women and members of underrepresented groups don't expand their networks sufficiently as they move up in their organizations. One reason is that the time spent cultivating new relationships, such as with other executives and external industry leaders, leaves less time for some of the important career connections made during earlier years. Some professionals feel guilty for leaving those connections behind. Others are pressured by members of their network to avoid establishing new relationships, since they might be accused of "becoming one of them." I'm not advocating that you ignore those individuals who supported your early successes, but at the same time, you can't be limited to those connections. You and your relationships need to change over time. The wider and stronger your network, the better poised you are to be a resource for others, including those connections you made earlier in your career.

AVOID "CONNECTION COMPROMISERS"

Your appearance and presence are an advertisement for why others should connect with you. Like in any branding campaign, your "packaging" often leads people to quickly decide whether or not they're interested in you. While I fully embrace the idea of being comfortable with who you are, it's important not to confuse a certain style of dress or appearance with the essence of who you are. Not long ago, a colleague of mine attended a one-man show about R. Buckminster Fuller, a rather eccentric twentieth-century genius most famous for the geodesic dome. He was years ahead of his time in his advocacy for green living. In the show, Fuller explained that in his earlier years, he was committed to wearing comfortable pants and shoes wherever he went—even social events that typically called for a suit and a tie. As you would expect, he got a lot of notice for his failure to conform to the social norms of the time. What he didn't get was funding for his novel ideas. Finally, Fuller said, "I decided to dress like a banker so that people could see *me* and my inventions, and not my eccentricities."

I was struck by his insight. Fuller might have felt more comfortable in khakis and sneakers; he might have thought formal dress requirements to be ostentatious. He also had the wisdom to see that his dress wasn't getting him the outcomes he wanted. In fact, it was distracting people from who he was and what he had to offer.

I encourage each of you to look at yourself with the same honesty. Are there things about the way you dress or present yourself that make it harder for others to connect with you? Does your presence suggest the strengths you bring to the table? The more approachable and appealing you make your "package," the more likely people will take the time to get to know you. This applies to your hair style, the clothes and jewelry you wear—even the way you talk. If your workplace is buttoned down and conservative, it's not the place for urban chic. There's a lot of truth in the adage, "Dress for the job you want, not the job you have." No matter how successful your efforts at the gym, dress in a manner that calls attention to your brains, not your body. If your language patterns are different from the people's whose positions you aspire to, consider adapting your grammar and vocabulary to reflect theirs.

> Does the way you dress or present yourself make it harder for others to connect with you?

I understand that dress, style of interaction, and language are controversial for many of us who are from different cultures. They become dividing lines between how much we conform to our work culture and how much we maintain our unique heritage and personal culture. Those are personal decisions. However, I encourage you to consider the outcomes you want and whether your decisions contribute to those outcomes.

If you choose to keep a style that's different from your organization's culture, then take personal responsibility for your decision; don't hide behind the intolerance of others. Own the fact that you must make the extra effort to build others' comfort with your choices and ensure that they don't make snap judgments based on your outward appearance. Some of you, like Fuller, will choose to buy the suit; others won't. The choice is yours, but don't blame others for the consequences of your choice.

I've been mentoring a young, talented, and ambitious black man. One day, he left me a message. He was contemplating an important decision and wanted my input. So urgent was his tone, I even stepped out of a meeting to take his call. I smiled to myself as he told me he was thinking about cutting off his dreadlocks because it would make him look "more like an executive." It was clear to me that his decision represented a turning point. He was declaring himself a player, someone who was ready to embrace the challenges of a leadership position in his organization. Changing his appearance indicated he knew that he belonged in that rank. It was a huge decision.

Interestingly, he did get more attention when the locks were gone. Could he have made it to the management team with his new confidence *and* his old hair style? I'm sure he could have. But by coming to terms with the fact that dreadlocks weren't an essential part of who he was—and that it conveyed a first impression that was different from the one he was trying to make in his organization—he removed an obstacle that could potentially get in his way and was clearly sending a message about his aspirations.

RELATIONAL CONFIDENCE DRAWS OTHERS TO YOU

You are the sum of your expertise, talents, and experience, not your clothes or your hair style or any other aspect of your outward appearance.

To make broad connections, you must draw people to you and not let them be distracted by labels.

Relationship building is a learned skill like any other skill. The more you practice, the better you become. You expand the range of personalities and perspectives that you can interact with gracefully. Your connections don't have to be limited to people like you. Rather, you build your confidence that you have something to offer in any relationship.

Confidence in relating to others sends a strong message. When I first started working on this book, I talked to many accomplished friends and colleagues about their own career journeys. Almost all of them could recount turning points in their careers that launched them on the trajectory to their current levels of success. I noticed that these pivotal moments were always more of an internal change rather than anything unique about the external circumstances.

Through a series of experiences—some positive, some more challenging—all of these individuals embraced who they were as people and what they had to offer. They realized they didn't have to be cookie-cutter versions of the people around them. They could connect to others from their unique heritage and perspective, but they didn't pigeonhole themselves—or let others pigeonhole them—based on their background. They were free to represent the full scope of their talents and perspectives. When they were comfortable with themselves and confident in their ability to relate to others, they were able to create more options for themselves. They leveraged their relationships to expand their impact.

Such freedom and confidence in your relational skills don't come easily, but the effort to learn to interact productively and build meaningful relationships across the broad spectrum of individuals is worth the payoff.

ADOPT KEY IDEAS

- Relational skills are as essential to your career success as the quality of your output. Building relationships is about securing the connections to grow your social capital; it is about your ability to exchange knowledge, guide the flow of information, and secure resources.

- Don't let discomfort drive your actions and cause you to miss an invaluable opportunity to make a connection. Become proactive and take the initiative in building relationships.

- Take the time to identify and internalize your value. Professionals who know their value are more likely to reach out and initiate connections.

- Effectively relating to others isn't about whether you like them or they like you. It's about figuring out the resources and support you and they have and how to work together to accomplish an objective.

- Make sure your presence suggests the strengths you bring to the table. The more approachable and appealing you make your package, the easier it is to establish connections.

BEGIN NOW

Prepare yourself to reach out and initiate a connection. Remember, the whole purpose of making a connection is to learn about that person and build comfort and trust. The connection lays the foundation for working together toward a shared objective.

- Identify the person you will connect with.
- Consider what you bring to the relationship. How might this person benefit from a connection with you?
- Determine how you will contact this person (for example, making a phone call, asking someone for an introduction, or attending an event). Then decide when you will initiate the connection.
- Prepare your introduction. Make sure your introduction leaves this person with the essence of your job, career interests, or personal attributes.

LEARN MORE

The Network Analysis is a tool that allows you to do a more in-depth assessment of your current network. You can download the assessment from *The Power of Choice* website (www.powerofchoice.net).

Efficacy graduate Kaplan Mobray's book, *The 10Ks of Personal Branding,* shows you how to represent yourself when you meet someone for the first time. Kaplan offers excellent advice on how to identify those things you want to be known for and offers a step-by-step approach for crafting an effective message that increases the likelihood you will be remembered.

USE INFLUENCE SKILLS TO SHAPE YOUR REALITY

The ultimate aim of this book is to enable you to shape the reality that's important to you—to proactively and deliberately pursue your goals—rather than have your future determined by the desires and motives of others. Everything I've talked about so far—building confidence, being resilient in the face of temporary setbacks or low expectations, studying the results of your efforts so you can become more effective, clearly identifying your desired outcome, and developing strategic relationships—is critical to your ability to engineer the professional life you desire.

The art of influencing others is so important to managing your career and to expanding your value to your organization that it, too, deserves special focus. This chapter explores how you command trust and respect without provoking fear or resentment. It examines how you become masterful at achieving the outcomes that are important to you and the work you do.

CHOOSE TO BE INFLUENTIAL

Making a conscious decision to be more influential is the first step—and often the most difficult. (See Figure 7-1.) When you become someone who shapes the opinions and practices of others, people begin to pay attention to you. You can't hide in the crowd. Others expect you to have an opinion and a strategy for action. They are also more likely to give you pushback on your ideas.

FIGURE 7-1: The Art of Influence

If you've been comfortable working in the background or relying on the decisions of others, it can be uncomfortable to take more control and to accept the responsibility of leadership. It can be especially uncomfortable for individuals whose differences make them feel they have to work harder to fit in or prove themselves. Many of us were taught to "go along to get along." Some of us were socialized to believe that we shouldn't share our opinions with those in authority or that we shouldn't challenge the perspectives of our coworkers. Still others feel that they are being too direct or aggressive when they advocate for themselves or a point of view. Because of these varying cultural messages, many professionals from diverse backgrounds often feel that it's less risky to let others set the tone and direction for important aspects of their work lives.

However, this perceived safety comes at a cost. If you don't offer opinions, people stop seeking them. If you don't take control of what happens to you, others decide for you. If you don't develop the skills to shape the commitment and effort of others, you become invisible to the movers and shakers within the organization. Over time, your career stagnates.

There are many ways to use influence skills effectively. Trust that there is an approach (or several approaches) that will fit your personality, your culture, and the needs of the situation. Some of you will learn to take bold stands in public settings; others will prefer to leverage opinions one-to-one in private conversations. Some of you will persuade through the power of writing; others will lead by example. Most likely, all of you will need to expand the repertoire you have now; you will have to step out of your comfort zones. To find the style of influence that works best for you, you must commit to building your capabilities in this area.

I'm reminded of four Asian women who attended an Efficacy program almost seven years ago. They were discouraged to realize that their strong cultural messages against self-promotion were contributing to their feelings of being stuck and taken for granted in their current positions. At the same time, they had a hard time imagining themselves giving the elevator speeches they had developed and practiced in the program. So they made a pact to stay in touch and help one another find ways to take credit for their accomplishments and convey their value to their organization. They encouraged each other to talk to their managers about their career goals, rather than waiting to be asked. They emboldened each other to reach out to other leaders to discuss their job function and what new responsibilities they'd be interested in. As they were offered new opportunities, they helped one another prepare for their interviews. Their hard work was very successful. By being intentional with their efforts to influence their careers, each of them has been promoted at least once; two of them have been promoted twice since they attended that Efficacy program.

> True power and far-reaching influence make an individual and those around him or her stronger.

In addition to the cultural messages you might have received about trying to influence others, there are other factors in many work environments that discourage the pursuit of influential proficiency. Influence skills might be labeled as manipulative. People are accused of brown-nosing or playing politics. Some use their influence to take advantage of others or to advance themselves at the expense of their colleagues. When you've witnessed or experienced such exploitation, it's understandable to be cautious about the use of power.

Influence built on manipulation and dishonesty has a shallow foundation—one that typically falls apart in the face of influence built from genuine alliances of mutual respect. True power and far-reaching influence make an individual *and those around him or her* stronger.

All organizations need influencers who can gain access to necessary resources or who can mobilize a group of people to get things done. There need to be leaders (formal or informal) who can facilitate a group's effort to solve problems and make a difference. It is only through developing influential proficiency that you have the power to better yourself and those around you.

As I said earlier, the first step in developing strong influence skills is deciding you want to be an influencer: you are willing to take the risk of the greater visibility and the greater expectations for leadership that come with the decision. Your payoff will be the increased control and freedom that comes from knowing how to engineer the outcomes you desire.

INFLUENCE SKILLS REQUIRE PRACTICE AND EFFORT

You have to decide you want to influence, and you have to trust that you *can* learn to influence. It has always struck me as odd that no one expects to immediately know how to program a computer or analyze a spreadsheet. Yet we often assume that some individuals are naturally persuasive and influential, that they are born leaders. Influence is like any other skill—perfecting it takes practice. Grasping how to influence others requires exposure to an increasing complexity of influence situations. Just as you can't learn how to play music without picking up an instrument, you can't learn how to exert influence without putting yourself in situations that require you to shape the opinions and behaviors of others. It takes commitment to trying different strategies in order to discover which ones are most effective in particular situations. Influence skills, like all areas of development, can be learned.

Some of us start practicing our influence skills at a very early age. I'm the oldest of five children. My siblings can attest that I regularly tried to persuade them to share *my* chores and *their* toys. As some of us get older, we use the skills we have developed to become high-school class officers or leaders in campus organizations. If you are one of these folks, trust that you can transfer those skills to the influence demands of the workplace. If you aren't, it's never too late to learn.

Begin by studying how things happen in your organization, both formally and informally. How do effective influencers create a shared vision and commitment? How do they present their point of view in a way that invites collaboration and agreement? How do they handle differing points of view?

Then take an incremental approach. Share your opinions more regularly in conversations with your friends. Offer your point of view to your manager. Speak up in meetings. Or offer to lead a small project. You can't wait to be given a title or permission to be a person of influence. Every work situation has opportunities to suggest an improvement, voice your interests, or motivate others to act. Begin to take advantage of them.

Pick a few situations where you'd like to have a bigger impact and jump in. Be willing to experiment with a variety of approaches. Some people need the facts and a good logical argument to be persuaded. Others need to identify with your vision. Still others are willing to go along in return for your support on something important to them. Learn from what's effective and what falls short. Ask for feedback and coaching from someone you trust to help refine your skills. Your willingness to stretch yourself and risk disagreement or rejection will teach you more about influencing than hiding yourself and your ideas. Your successes will give you confidence and increase your comfort in shaping the attitudes and actions of others—the essence of influence.

IDENTIFY YOUR DESIRED OUTCOME

As with any area of effective effort, you have to be clear about the outcome you want before you try to influence a situation. You have to know the goal you're moving toward in order to gauge whether you're having an impact—and where you are willing to negotiate. Be open to the possibility that there are likely several ways to achieve your goal, not just the solution you have in mind. Be willing to back up or take some detours when you need to, but stay focused on your desired outcome.

Recently, an employee came to me asking to cut back on the projects she was responsible for. I didn't have other folks who could step in and take on some of her workload; we were all stretched thin. So as much as I wanted to be sympathetic, I wasn't too pleased with her request, and I'm sure I conveyed that. She revealed that a big source of tension was feeling immense pressure to respond immediately to the e-mails I send out at all hours of the day and night. (I travel a lot, so nights and weekends are my time for reaching out to internal folks.) She never felt like she could be "off" when she was working on projects with me.

With that understanding, we were able to work out a mutually agreeable solution. She would acknowledge my request within twenty-four hours and let me know when she would be able to complete it. We both went away satisfied with the outcome. I know she's working on what's important to me even if I don't get an immediate response, and she's more in control of when and how she works. Because she could identify that having more control over her schedule—not necessarily a reduction of her responsibilities—was most important to her, it was easier to find a mutually agreeable solution.

IDENTIFY THE BENEFITS

Influence happens best in the context of a relationship. To earn support for your ideas and approaches, you have to show that you'll support the objectives of those you most want to influence. The best influencers don't concentrate on pushing their point of view. They concentrate on figuring out why someone might be willing to adopt their perspective or approach. They make those benefits clear to those they want to influence. They've learned that talking more or louder doesn't usually change people's minds. (If the influencer is in a position of power, it might change behavior temporarily, but simply pushing an opinion more aggressively seldom results in a change of heart.)

Being a good influencer requires being a good observer and a good listener. What does the other person have to gain by adopting your approach? What are they concerned about? How can you protect their interests while advancing your own?

Our clients, like all customers, want to know that they are getting a good return on the investment they make in their business relationship with Global Novations. I learned a long time ago that when I clearly position our services as an answer to a client's problems—a way to increase productivity or reduce turnover costs, for

> When you encounter a lack of support, it means you haven't made the case for why your recommended approach is in the other's best interest.

example—the client is much less concerned about the cost. In order to make my solutions convincing, however, I have to really understand the source of the client's pain and offer an approach that provides relief. If I were to push a product for the sake of our revenue numbers, the client would see through that right away. This is true in any influence situation: it has to be clear that the influencer has the interests of the other party at heart before that person is willing to collaborate or offer support.

All influencers encounter a lack of support from others at times. When this happens to you, understand that at its core, any resistance is seldom really about you. Rather, you haven't made the case for why your recommended approach or desired outcome is in the interest of whomever you're trying to influence. The person you're trying to influence is anticipating some cost—in time, money, inconvenience, or esteem, for example—that you haven't convinced them is worth paying. To be successful in your approach, you have to figure out the win for the other person.

UNDERSTAND THE CONTEXT OF THE SITUATION

Many influence situations are like icebergs: you can see some of the problem, but in most situations there's much more underneath the surface. Just as it was the ice underneath the surface that sank the *Titanic*, failing to consider the more hidden aspects of any negotiation or influence situation can derail your efforts.

Study the unwritten rules in your organization. How do effective influencers shape the willing collaboration of others? For instance, in many organizations, the real decision making is seldom done in group meetings. Opinions are shaped one conversation at a time well before the meeting where the official decision gets made. You can have the best proposal, but if you haven't built support for it ahead of time, it's unlikely to get accepted.

In any negotiation or influence situation, you also have to calculate what's possible. You have to understand the cost of the position you're taking. There are some situations where the cost of negotiation is high, and being inflexible damages your credibility as an influencer. The most effective influencers learn to assess which situations are moderate risks and which are unrealistic (for now).

For instance, I was coaching an individual about setting better boundaries between his workload and his personal commitments. This was a person who believed he had to say yes to everything, so we were working on prioritizing those responsibilities that yielded the best return. He had identified client contact opportunities as his first priority. As a result, when he was asked to attend a high-profile internal training program open only to folks who were seen as having high potential, he asked the program coordinator for a rain check since the date conflicted with a big client conference he had been invited to attend as a participant. To make matters worse, he gave little explanation about why he declined the invitation. Although I applauded his efforts to be more strategic in how he spends his time, he failed to calculate the cost. The invitation to attend the internal training was seen as a real plum; declining it cost him a significant level of support from the manager who had proposed his nomination.

It might have been possible to negotiate another opportunity for the training; it certainly was possible to negotiate other opportunities for client interaction. But because this individual didn't fully calculate the cost of asking for a rain check, he didn't influence the situation in a way that was aligned with his best interests.

I've seen people champion a worthwhile cause—the organization's approach to inclusion, an improved work process, or a new product—and become frustrated, derailed, and dismissed because they expected change at a pace the organization wasn't ready to adopt. Then, instead of focusing on how to shape incremental progress, they lost their credibility by being righteous about their expectations for change, rather than strategic in the steps required to ultimately prevail. The best influencers don't settle for the status quo; they always believe they can make a difference. But they also pay close attention to the best opportunities to use their leverage and work at influencing change in stages.

BUILD ALLIANCES WITH PEOPLE WHO HAVE INFLUENCE

As your span of influence expands, you can't personally influence every individual whose support makes a difference. You need to have connections with others who will help shape your desired outcomes.

Understand that these alliances need to extend in all directions within the organization. Often, people on the front line can just as quickly sabotage the effective implementation of a good idea as someone who is higher up. They might not be able to pull the plug on a budget, but they can certainly make costly mistakes or ignore the effort entirely. On the flip side, the ability to influence the discretionary efforts of those you rely on for executing critical projects expands your contribution to the organization exponentially. You are not only contributing your own efforts but also the efforts of those you influence.

In the previous chapter, we talked about networking—getting to know people and having them get to know you. Building an alliance is a higher-order relationship. It's when two people have worked together enough to understand their shared interests, and they agree to work on each other's behalf in order to accomplish an individual goal. Each side knows what they have to gain by collaborating and what they have to lose by conflict.

At one point in my career, the CEO of my company was adamant that we needed to accelerate the time frame in which our most promising talent became officers. He charged me with designing a process that would reduce the development time for an officer from the typical ten to fifteen years to five years. This was a task with many obstacles. There was understandable internal resistance to the notion that we would select a limited number of people for a targeted development experience. And there was skepticism that it was possible to create an effective officer in only five years. I knew that if any accelerated track were going to be effective, it had to have the buy-in of the line leadership, or else those selected would not receive the internal support required to ensure they had the appropriate experience and business savvy.

Before I began planning how to structure the program, I had extensive conversations with the various officers. I learned about their interests so I could win their support. For some, it was simply understanding that this project was important to the CEO. Others saw it as a means of more aggressively growing our business. When I had the backing of enough leaders to establish the credibility of the effort, I proceeded with designing the details: how we would handle the selection process, which schools we would tap for an accelerated MBA experience, and the developmental rotations that would be critical.

Had I been given this assignment earlier in my career, I think I would have erroneously believed that because the CEO charged me with making this happen, I could go ahead and put a process in place. Fortunately, by the time I had to take on this project, I had learned the importance of building alliances. I knew I had to build support and credibility for the overall idea—and for the specifics of the implementation—so that the rising officers would be legitimately positioned for success.

INFLUENCE IS NOT ASKING FOR PERMISSION

There is a subtle, but very important, distinction in the attitudes of the most effective influencers. Effective influencers believe they have *the power* and *the right* to advocate for what's important to them. They are appropriately respectful of authority, they are cognizant of the current limitations and challenges in any situation, and they understand the critical importance of others' buy-in. However, they don't ask for others' permission to pursue what's important to them. They *give themselves permission*—and then proceed to devise a strategy for gathering the resources and support necessary to accomplish their goals. Instead of thinking, "They won't let me," they think, "What do I need to do next?" This fundamental belief—*I have the right and the capacity to shape my circumstances*—causes a profound shift in the quality of one's influence efforts. It places the power for change squarely with the individual rather than abdicating that power to others.

> **Effective influencers believe they have the power and the right to advocate for what's important to them.**

Own the power to be an effective influencer. Developing your influence skills is at the heart of achieving the professional career that's important to you. If you don't shape your own circumstances, someone else will. How to exert influence is a learnable skill. Whatever level of influence expertise you have now—whether it's refined and far-reaching or still rudimentary—commit to expanding your ability to make things happen for yourself and for others. Every one of us has opportunities to practice and learn how to tap the willing support of others *if* we choose to be intentional about expanding our breadth and depth of influence.

ADOPT KEY IDEAS

- Decide you want to become more influential. The payoff will be the increased control and freedom that comes from knowing how to engineer the outcomes that are important to you.
- Be clear about what you want as an outcome, and be open to the possibility that there are likely several ways to achieve your goal.
- Identify the benefits for the other person; why might he or she be willing to adopt your perspective or approach?
- Create change over time; assess which situations are moderate risks and which situations are unrealistic for now.
- Build alliances with other influencers so that you expand your power to accomplish shared goals.

BEGIN NOW

Identify a situation where you feel your influence would benefit those involved. It should be one that will require you to stretch your influence skills but where you have confidence you can make a difference.

- Identify the outcome you want.
- Identify the benefits for those involved. Why should they adopt your perspective or approach?
- Think through how you will approach the situation. What actions or points of discussion on your part are likely to influence others?
- Discuss your approach with someone you trust, and ask for feedback.

- Study the outcome of your effort to understand your results. Remember to own the success of your effort and look for ways to improve your impact in the future.

LEARN MORE

Use the Global Novations Listener Analysis Profile to identify the needs and concerns of those you want to influence. You can access the tool from *The Power of Choice* website (www.powerofchoice.net).

PART III
EFFICACY IN ACTION

REAL-WORLD EXAMPLES

The principles of Efficacy offer a perspective for managing the many choices you have to make—and the many obstacles you will encounter—in the course of a demanding and fulfilling career. More than a prescriptive set of actions, they serve as a compass that guides your response to circumstances and helps you create the environment you want to work in.

The scenarios on the following pages are examples of real-life situations encountered by professionals who consider themselves, or are considered by others, to be different. Some details have been altered to protect confidentiality, but you will recognize their dilemmas. Some scenarios portray difficult situations that many professionals find themselves in and how they typically react. Others are examples of individuals managing challenges in ways that enabled them to accomplish their desired outcomes.

After each example, I ask several questions about what's happening in each scenario and what would be an effective response given the person's challenges. I encourage you to think about these questions before jumping ahead to my analysis and recommendations. Doing so will build your

Efficacy "muscle" and help you to think critically about the best approach for your own circumstances.

In addition to offering a perspective on each example, I also comment on how you might more broadly apply the principles used in that particular situation. My comments aren't intended to offer the definitive way to respond. The purpose is to help you anticipate and choose responses that will help you manage your career by design, not by default.

NO PROMOTION, LITTLE FEEDBACK

In the five years that Chen has been with his company, he has worked diligently, met every deadline, and consistently fulfilled expectations. He is well-liked by his colleagues, and on occasion his boss has commented that he is an excellent team player and the backbone of the group due to his competence and reliability.

Despite all that, Chen is frustrated. The senior staff doesn't seem to notice him; he feels like he fades into the background. Although he has led a few projects, Chen has never been asked to head up any critical client engagements. Chen is troubled every time he reflects on the fact that after five years he still has not become a manager. He doesn't understand why four others who joined the company at the same time he did have already been promoted.

Last year during his performance review, when Chen asked what he needed to do to get a top rating, his boss merely replied, "Don't worry. You're doing fine. You're a solid performer." Chen didn't push the issue. He just sat quietly in his frustration.

Recently Chen complained to his wife, "My boss must be blind! I don't know why he can't see my value to the company. I'm well-liked by the others on the team, and without question, my technical skills are much stronger than the guy they just promoted to manager."

REFLECTION QUESTIONS

- What might Chen need to do differently to position himself for promotion to manager?
- In his performance review, how could Chen have responded to his boss in order to receive meaningful feedback?
- What is a next step Chen could take to regain career momentum?

ANALYSIS AND RECOMMENDATIONS

Chen has two problems. First, he assumes that the technical skills that made him successful as an individual contributor and team member are the same set of competencies required for management. He has mistakenly believed that by working hard in his current job, he would move up. Second, he's not receiving information about what he needs to do differently in order to be promoted.

It's hard for Chen to take control of his development since he's not focusing on the right issues and he doesn't have the benefit of direct and constructive feedback. Although it's true that a company might sometimes promote an individual because he or she is excellent in a current position, in this case, it seems likely that the manager is looking for evidence that Chen has the potential to be effective in a new and different kind of role.

Chen should determine the skills a manager needs. One way to do that is to study the behaviors of those who are being promoted (instead of assuming he is being unfairly overlooked). With a better understanding of the skills and behaviors that are required, Chen would be better able to choose activities that build or demonstrate his competence in those areas. For instance, he might ask his manager to take the lead on a project team or offer his ideas in team meetings more directly. He might take advantage of his technical expertise and volunteer to coach a newer member of the team.

It's also clear that Chen's boss is either uncomfortable with giving direct feedback or doesn't know how. A next step for Chen could be to encourage his boss to be more open and provide in-depth and thoughtful—rather than superficial and cursory—feedback. For instance, instead of being silent when he receives vague reassurances, Chen could make it clear he wants to be promoted (not just receive top performance ratings).

He should ask specifically about the skills he needs to develop in order to position himself for a management opportunity.

THE BROADER APPLICATION

Although you can comb your hair or shave without looking in a mirror, the mirror makes the process much easier, faster, and effective. That's what feedback does for our development. Without quality feedback, development can become a laborious trial-and-error process.

How to Encourage Feedback

If, like Chen, you're not receiving the feedback you need, make sure you're treating it like a gift—a special contribution toward your growth. Ask yourself if you're truly open to hearing others' opinions and advice. Do you make it safe for them to tell you their real assessment of your skills and potential for additional responsibility? Do you ignore or dismiss the feedback, or do you listen and use the information to accelerate your growth? Managers and colleagues will be more inclined to tell you what you need to hear if they see evidence that you put the feedback to good use. In addition, don't be defensive if you receive feedback you don't like or don't agree with. Even if you have a different assessment of your skills or situation, knowing others' opinions gives you more control over influencing the outcome you want.

Ask yourself if you're truly open to hearing others' opinions and advice.

Sometimes you have to change your approach in order to receive feedback. You might have to build a stronger relationship of trust with your boss, ask more direct questions, be clear about the kind of information you're looking for, or ask your manager to be direct and honest about how you're perceived relative to the standards and expectations. Especially in situations where you've lost momentum, you need a clear and practical understanding—not a vague sense—of the steps you need to take.

If necessary, find other sources for feedback. For instance, connect with a mentor, or network with those who have been successful in reaching goals similar to yours. Avoid the temptation to seek out feedback that is reassuring but doesn't give you any hard data about how you can be more effective.

Employ Effective Effort

If you're not getting the outcome you want, especially after a period of time, that in and of itself is feedback: there's something about your approach you need to change. If you don't receive a promotion (or another desired outcome), you can be sure there's a disconnect between what you want and the support others are willing to give you to accomplish it. Your job is to seek out the information that will enable you to engineer a different result. Then you have to be willing to take the steps that are necessary to truly grow and develop. This could mean a lateral move. It could mean taking on different kinds of projects. It could mean recruiting a coach or mentor. But you must do something differently in order to get a different outcome.

Expand Your Contribution over Time

Regardless of whether or not you want to be promoted, in order to continue to be highly valued by your organization, you need to change the way you contribute over the course of your career. The work you do should expand in complexity and importance. Look for opportunities to use your expertise to solve more demanding problems over time. If your contribution doesn't change (and especially if your salary does), you run the risk of being seen as someone who is not quite worth the level of investment the company is making in you.

Those who are most valued also expand their sphere of influence. Instead of continuing to contribute only through their own effort, they become individuals who support others to work effectively—either through their coaching and leadership as a manager or as a team member that others come to for support and guidance. They look for opportunities to have a strategic impact: How can the organization work more efficiently? What new products or processes could it implement? How could it serve its customers better?

You don't necessarily have to change jobs in order to change the way you contribute; you do have to consider how you can increase your impact on the organization's success. For instance, our receptionist at Global Novations was responsible for reconciling the FedEx invoices. She noticed that almost all packages were being sent for overnight delivery, even those that were not urgent. She compiled a table that showed the costs and delivery times for various delivery methods—UPS, the United States Postal Service, and FedEx—and distributed it as a tool for making the most cost-efficient choice for sending packages. Global Novations decreased its shipping costs by 20 percent the following year—a significant contribution from our receptionist.

When you understand the need to expand the way you contribute over time, like this receptionist, you are more likely to be alert to opportunities that will grow your expertise across all dimensions—technically, relationally, and influentially. You will be better positioned for promotion, should you desire upward advancement, and more highly valued as an individual contributor if you don't want to pursue a leadership track.

MANAGING LOW EXPECTATIONS

Upon graduating with her MBA, Shaniqua was hired by a prestigious investment firm and entered its one-year management-development program along with other newly hired MBAs. Her group consisted of ten people that would go through three fifteen-week rotations over the course of a year in order to gain exposure to key functions in the firm.

Shaniqua was a highly confident individual and a real go-getter from Washington, DC. She had a big smile, an engaging personality, dressed in bright African-style fabrics, and wore her hair in multiple long braids.

During these rotations, partners generally reach out to help those in the program learn the culture of the company. Occasionally, a partner invites a member of the group out to lunch or offers additional coaching and informal feedback. Ryan, one of Shaniqua's cohorts, had this experience. A partner took Ryan under his wing, which seemed to give Ryan momentum. Shaniqua often heard that partner telling Ryan, "You remind me of me when I started with the firm."

Shaniqua's experience was a stark contrast to that. None of the partners reached out to her. In fact, Shaniqua felt that the partners overlooked her or interacted with her only as needed. When assignments were distributed, it seemed to her that she always got the weakest or most boring projects. It was almost as if they didn't expect much from her. She got little coaching, and if she got any feedback at all from a partner, it was vague and conveyed in a somewhat negative in tone: "Your written communication is not as clear as we need it to be. I'm sure you're doing the best you can. Try doing a rewrite. When you get bogged down, I have an open-door policy. So come see me, and I will do what I can to help you get you back on track."

By the end of the first rotation, Shaniqua was frustrated and angry about the firm. She complained to a friend, "Initially, I thought this would be a good place to start a career, but I've been having some real doubts about whether I can be successful here. It's unusual to see an African American in the firm, let alone an African-American woman. This firm has a big push around recruiting diversity, but I don't think they're serious about giving folks like me a real chance to succeed."

Halfway through the second rotation, she missed a deadline on a project. Recounting the incident later, Shaniqua commented, "I was so embarrassed. That partner yelled at me in front of everyone at the project meeting. He insinuated that I was not his choice for his team, but that he was stuck with me because the management-development program made the assignment."

Shaniqua found herself avoiding colleagues on the project team who had witnessed the partner's tirade. She also skipped several of the Friday evening get-togethers with her cohorts from the management-development program. She knew these were intended as opportunities to relax, blow off steam, and offer one another support, but Shaniqua complained to her family, "They keep asking me how I feel about my job. They ask me about my background, my social life—they keep trying to get into my business. I am annoyed at how nosy these people are."

Shaniqua finally shared with her family that she was considering quitting before the next rotation started: "I'm not cut out to be in an investment firm. Why would anyone want to work in such a boring industry anyway? I think I should shift to something completely different."

REFLECTION QUESTIONS

- In what ways were low expectations communicated to Shaniqua?
- What do you think triggered the low expectations?
- To what extent did Shaniqua accept and internalize those expectations?
- At what points in Shaniqua's story could she have responded differently to keep herself from going into a downward spiral?

ANALYSIS AND RECOMMENDATIONS

Shaniqua got caught in a downward spiral of low expectations. Regardless of whether the low expectations were triggered by discomfort with her or by stereotyped assumptions about her, they still had a significant impact on her confidence and performance. When she wasn't supported or challenged to expand her expertise, she began to withdraw. Her efforts to deliver strong outcomes were compromised. Since she wasn't as engaged as her colleagues, it's likely that her withdrawal reinforced the original low expectations. She also allowed her anger and disappointment to get in the way of using the support her colleagues could have offered.

It's understandably frustrating when others react to you because of your difference. Shaniqua's race, dress, hair—even her name—might have caused discomfort with her. Unfortunately, people tend to avoid individuals and situations that make them uncomfortable, and that avoidance leads to little or no feedback and low expectations.

Although I'm not justifying that behavior, Shaniqua should acknowledge that her differences might be an obstacle in establishing rapport and trust with the firm's partners. Then she needs to ask herself whether she'd rather be a victim of circumstances or look for ways to take control. If she wants to be treated like Ryan, she will need to be proactive to reduce the "noise" that her appearance and name might cause. Even something as simple as, "Hello, I'm Shaniqua; don't be afraid to mispronounce my name" can go a long way in making a connection and establishing a level of comfort that will jump-start a relationship.

It's absolutely critical that Shaniqua stay engaged. Although she was understandably upset by her manager's public criticism of her, she needs to be proactive to figure out his expectations and shape his perception of her contributions. She might have asked for a meeting with him to better understand how she can deliver to the standards and to deepen his awareness of her expertise.

She could also have an honest conversation with a colleague or mentor about how she sees the situation and ask for advice on how to interact more effectively. Blaming or judging others isn't likely to produce the outcome she wants. If she can be openly curious about how she might interact with others to receive the assignments and support she wants, she gives others insight into her goals and invites them to engage with her.

THE BROADER APPLICATION

Although it's certainly demoralizing when you have to confront low expectations or lack of support from others, keep your focus on what you can control. When you withdraw or put your energy into blaming others, you compromise your capacity to engineer the backing and opportunities necessary to advance your career.

Create Comfort and Build Trust

Being able to effectively create comfort and build trust is a critical interpersonal skill set for women and minority professionals. Too often, we assume we have no control over others' reactions to us; our energy is focused on the bias and insensitivity of others.

Start with the assumption that you have the power and the capacity to make meaningful connections with others. Accept the fact that it will take work—maybe even more work than for some of your colleagues—to build connections. However, the alternative is to let your possibilities be limited by others' discomfort with you. Some professionals choose to conform to the people and organizations around them in order to accomplish what's important to them. Others maintain a very unique style. However, all of them who are influential are intentional in their efforts to relate well to others and to help others become familiar and comfortable with them.

It's Not the Stimulus, It's the Response

All of us hit periods in our careers where we stumble or where we're pressed to prove our capabilities to others. The trick is to catch yourself when the challenges begin to result in a downward spiral. When you find yourself feeling helpless or blaming others for your difficulties, take a step back and ask yourself what you can do to protect your confidence and move toward a better outcome.

Refuse to be a victim of the circumstances around you.

Assume you're not a victim of the circumstances around you. Strong performance outcomes begin with confidence. Confidence can be built up or eroded, so connect yourself with people who believe in you and provide support. When caught in a downward spiral, reach out for help to break the cycle. Seek out mentors, colleagues, or friends you trust who will give you the support you need. Look for those who can provide perspectives and strategies that will help you get grounded again.

Then reshape your approach by employing effective effort. Remember that effective effort is characterized by being seriously committed and engaged, focused on receiving feedback, and strategic in using that feedback to learn and improve outcomes. When you deliver strong outcomes, you add value to the business. You build the "personal equity" that can move people beyond assumptions about you and focus attention on your expertise, not your differences.

MAKING WORK-LIFE CHOICES

R ani was a successful senior project manager for a high-tech company specializing in robotic system implementations. Her role often required long hours and much travel. She was generally regarded as the top project manager in the organization and on the fast track toward a leadership role.

Fifteen months ago, Rani and her husband, Arun, had a baby girl. The career-driven couple suddenly became a family, and this created a new set of competing values and priorities. Rani had never envisioned herself as a stay-at-home mom, yet she felt the daily internal tug-of-war between wanting to achieve excellence at work and a strong desire to spend more time at home with her daughter.

Rani and Arun decided that she should explore other options that would not require her to travel. At her mid-year review with Trent, her director, she shared her concerns: "You know how committed I am to this work and to our company. Clients continually request me for each new implementation. Currently, I am managing a project in Seattle, one in Boston, and successfully wrapping one up in London. Right now, the key challenge for me is the extensive travel. As a new mom, I need to reduce the amount of travel in order to achieve some level of work-life balance."

Rani was relieved when Trent reacted positively. He said that although her work was fine, she seemed to be more stressed and less energized by it. He assured her that he didn't want to lose her as part of his team, and he would see what he could do to make this work for her.

Three weeks later, Trent came back with a solution. It was a lateral move in the department to become the regulatory/compliance manager. It required no travel and would allow Rani to work from home two days a week. In this role she would no longer have any direct reports and her focus would be to generate internal and external reports and interface with project teams via phone or e-mail.

Trent emphasized to Rani that her project expertise would add value in dealing with compliance issues. But he also cautioned her about her career prospects: "You know I've been positioning you on the management fast track because you are my best project manager. However, while you are in this job, I won't be able to champion you for promotion up the leadership ladder."

After only nine months in the regulatory/compliance role, Rani had established herself as a subject matter expert, yet she felt conflicted and increasingly restless. The lack of travel and being at home with her daughter was great, but Rani missed the challenge and the thrill of working on high-visibility, international implementations, leading teams, and impressing clients. She had understood that this role would pull her off the fast track, but now all sorts of assumptions were being made about what she was and wasn't willing to do. As she conveyed to one of Global Novations' coaches, "Recently there were a few great local assignments that I could have run with, but because of the potential time demands, I wasn't even asked. It stinks that the organization has pigeonholed me on the mommy track and I've dropped off the radar. I didn't sign up for that."

REFLECTION QUESTIONS

- What do you think would represent "work-life balance" for Rani?
- To what extent did Rani get the outcomes she wanted by taking this new position?
- What are the key sources of Rani's frustration and anger? Where do you think she is placing the blame?
- Given the realities of her new position, what could she be doing differently to manage how she is viewed in the organization?

ANALYSIS AND RECOMMENDATIONS

Rani is now in an unchallenging job and full of regret that she slowed down her career and is no longer on the promotion track. She feels torn between being home with her family and being chal-lenged. Although there is some truth to "you can't have it all"—at least not all at the same time—you don't necessarily have to make an all-or-nothing deci-sion. When Rani's boss found a job for her that did not require travel and allowed her to work from home, she simply accepted his solution.

With a credible track record and the support of her manager, Rani could have leveraged her value more.

Either Rani did not fully anticipate the tradeoffs or is unwilling to live with the realities of her decision. In order to make strong decisions about what constitutes work-life harmony for herself, Rani needs to be honest about what is most important to her at this phase of life. Traveling internationally 85 percent of the time did not afford her any flexibility and time with her family. Yet her current lackluster, unchal-lenging role is neither satisfying nor a career she is proud of.

Rani was a strong performer with a very credible track record and the support of her manager. She should have leveraged her value much more than she did to explore options that could have better integrated her skills with her desire to be more available to her family. For instance, although her boss couldn't support her for promotion while on the mommy track, she could have done a better job in positioning herself prior to the job change by making it clear she wanted to pick up the pace of her career again in a year or two. She could have been more proactive in working with her boss to shape a position that would allow her to cut back on her travel yet stay in a management track. Or she could have leveraged her network to find other options for herself, other than the one Trent offered.

THE BROADER APPLICATION

When asking for an accommodation, we sometimes assume we must accept whatever is offered. We fall into a default mode and allow people to take care of us and make defining decisions. Often we're so grateful for the job flexibility, we hesitate to come back and ask for more responsibility or negotiate reentry.

Manage Your Career by Design, Not by Default

Do not assume that you have only one option. Be proactive in shaping your outcomes. Be clear about what you want as a result, leverage a clear value proposition, and use your influence strategies and power to make things happen. Don't let others make the decision for you.

Strong Contributions Give You Negotiating Power

It is your value to the company that gives you negotiating room in the first place. The more you deliver strong outcomes and expand the ways in which you contribute to the business, the more power you have in creating flexibility for yourself.

However, I've observed that many women (and some men) take themselves out of the game too soon and slow down their career momentum. They begin disengaging even when they are just thinking about starting a family, or they fail to position themselves for effective reentry. They opt out of career-developing opportunities because they fear it will be harder to pull back when they choose to have children. Unfortunately, they end up limiting their options more than they need to. As Sheryl Sandburg, the COO of Facebook, said in a TEDTalk titled "Why We

Have Too Few Women Leaders," "Don't leave, before you leave." The greater your value to the company, the more power you will have to negotiate a changed role for those years during which you might want to give a greater balance of your time and energy to your personal life.

DEALING WITH
A DIFFICULT BOSS

After only eighteen months with the company, Ricardo stood out as a motivated self-starter with a good eye for detail. Managers and colleagues liked the fact that he could take something and run with it on his own from start to finish. His technical expertise positioned him to join a high-profile process-implementation group, long known for its strong teamwork. Joining this team was viewed as a step up for anyone in engineering, which fueled Ricardo's pride and excitement.

Lauren, the director of the group, was known for her straightforward, no-nonsense leadership style. She was often described as intensely driven, technically talented, politically astute, and definitely on the leadership fast track. Ricardo was determined to impress Lauren as his new boss.

Within the first month, however, Lauren's brusque personality and hands-on approach began frustrating Ricardo. She asked to review everything he did before it went to a client. But what annoyed him most was that she always made revisions to his work. It was never good enough.

Lauren also ran Ricardo's work by the team for its suggestions. Although this was her practice for all team members, in Ricardo's mind this just added insult to injury. Ricardo complained to a friend, "It's one thing to have my boss tear apart my work, but to invite others to take shots at me . . . I get the feeling that I'm an easy target being the only Hispanic in the group. It's as if they don't expect my work to be any good. A few of my new colleagues took me to lunch to offer support, but I'm not sure I believe all the talk about trust and teamwork. After all, they never seem to pass up an opportunity to critique my work."

For the last report he prepared, Lauren suggested he add a few more charts and graphs. Ricardo argued that this was overkill, but she insisted he change it. To Ricardo, this was an example of Lauren exerting her power simply because she could, which he thought she did frequently. For instance, she typically rushed into team meetings late and then asked endless, detailed questions. To Ricardo, this was way too much time to spend simply to satisfy Lauren's need for control.

Although Lauren was the most difficult boss he ever had, Ricardo knew he needed to make this work. He decided to talk with Lauren about the impact of her management style on his work and dropped by her office to broach the subject. It took a few minutes for her to even look up from her computer, but once she finally acknowledged him, Ricardo began to spill out his frustration about her hands-on style: "I feel like I am stuck between a rock and a hard place. You give me little freedom to operate, so I cannot bring my best work to the table. You don't give me a chance to shine."

Lauren was quick to respond: "Our team is known for its unique style and high standards. Obviously you don't get it yet. Eventually you will see the wisdom of our team's culture and get the hang of things around here—or perhaps you can find a team that fits your style better." Before Ricardo could say another word, Lauren was back at her computer. He felt shut down and dismissed.

Since then, Ricardo has kept his distance from Lauren and avoided team assignments in favor of tasks that he could accomplish on his own.

REFLECTION QUESTIONS

- Where do you place the responsibility for this difficult work relationship?
- What blind spots does Ricardo have in interpreting his interactions with Lauren and the team?
- What could Ricardo do to improve his relationship with Lauren?

ANALYSIS AND RECOMMENDATIONS

Ricardo enjoyed operating as a lone ranger in his previous position and experienced success with that style. However, his current job requires a different kind of interaction. Unfortunately, Ricardo has focused on what doesn't work for him and what he doesn't like about Lauren's management style.

In order to create a better working relationship, Ricardo needs to start by considering Lauren's point of view. She has a highly successful team. She believes that her team is effective because of her high standards. She strives to improve her team's output by critiquing individuals' work, and she expects the members of the group to do the same for one another. Time is precious; she doesn't waste it.

> The burden of responsibility is on you to demonstrate your value and win your manager's trust and support.

Because he misunderstood—and ultimately passed judgment on—the team's culture of open feedback and collaboration, he failed to win Lauren's trust or secure the support of his team. He didn't see that his teammates were trying to give him feedback about how to work effectively in this environment rather than judging him because of his ethnicity. He failed to realize that his preference for working independently was causing him to lose out on valuable information about the expectations for the work output.

Ricardo has given Lauren little incentive to change a style that has been effective for her to suit the preferences of a newcomer, whom she likely sees as critical of her and resistant to feedback. Consider the way in which Ricardo set up the critical conversation about his frustration with

Lauren. Given her schedule and pace of working, she's not likely to be receptive to a serious conversation when he unexpectedly drops by her office. However, Ricardo didn't consider his own role in the reaction he got. He saw it as one more piece of evidence about how difficult Lauren is to work with.

The burden of responsibility is on Ricardo to understand and accommodate the prevalent style of the group before he advocates for any changes that might better fit his work style. He needs to establish trust and demonstrate that he can contribute to the group's success. He needs to show Lauren that he understands her expectations and will take advantage of the give-and-take process of the team to refine his work.

THE BROADER APPLICATION

If you want a key leader's attention and support, it is incumbent on you to see things from his or her perspective. You must give him or her a reason or incentive to invest in you.

Study the Culture

The same skills and work style that made you successful in one part of the organization might not be what is required in a different department, in a different role, or at a higher level within that same organization. In every new situation, you have to learn and adapt to the cultural nuances of that specific group or role. Too often, we are quick to criticize and judge, rather than seek to understand, the new environment. What is the logic behind the way things are done? What goals and values do you have in common with the new team? How can you adapt your work style to the culture of the group?

You can learn the hard way by trial and error, or you can accelerate your learning by building relationships with your manager and colleagues. You might not agree with their point of view about what supports the group to work most effectively, but you will be able to interact more strategically if you understand the culture.

Establish Your Value

You need to understand your value proposition from your manager's point of view. Get on your boss's wavelength and determine what's important to him or her. You are not going to be supported to do your best work if you're seen as someone who resists the "way things are done" or expends a lot of energy blaming or criticizing others.

This is not to say that you must always accept the status quo. In fact, part of your value proposition in a new situation is that you bring new perspectives and expertise. However, when you make it clear to your manager that you understand the prevailing culture, and that your intention is to support him or her and the team, you are in a better position to sell your new idea and fresh approach.

Before recommending a change, articulate your understanding of the team's objectives and how you see yourself contributing to the achievement of those goals. Then you can position your recommendations or request for a different kind of support as something that will enhance your contribution. Finally, always ask for input: is your suggestion something your manager can support? When it's clear you're aligned with what's important to your manager and open to feedback, you are much more likely to get a receptive response.

NOT CONNECTING
IN INDIANA

From the time Colin joined the regional office in San Jose, California, his career quickly gained momentum. His technical expertise and ability to troubleshoot issues at client sites earned him recognition as a go-to person. After only two years with the company, Colin was made a project leader and was being positioned for a move into management. He told his mentor, "I like the company, its people, and the work. It seems a perfect fit, given my skills and interests." Colin's mentor had already encouraged him to seriously consider opportunities at corporate headquarters in the Midwest, because it would be the perfect next step for a long-term career with the company.

Eight months later, Colin accepted a junior management position at headquarters in Indiana. This would be a huge transition for this native Californian, but Colin was comforted by the fact that Ken, his partner of five years, was willing to move.

The new job was just the challenge Colin had hoped for. Corporate headquarters was large, but it had a solid on-boarding process. Colin found the people professional and polite, but somewhat standoffish. Patricia, a senior manager, was assigned as Colin's mentor and "buddy" for the first three months. She introduced him to his coworkers, explained the corporate culture, and gave him a heads-up on some of the unwritten rules. However, after the three months were up, he didn't hear from her. Joel, Colin's new boss, was often behind closed doors, but he occasionally stopped by Colin's office and made himself available for questions. Colin felt like he had a good working relationship with Joel, even if they didn't interact regularly.

His coworkers seemed more ill at ease with him, which Colin assumed was related to his being gay. He had been surprised at the relative absence of a gay and lesbian employee group and how hidden gays were in the community in general. Being new to headquarters and not having the support of a gay network in the company or community, Colin chose to be very discreet at work so as not to make others uncomfortable. He never talked about Ken or brought him to company functions or informal gatherings after work. Over time, this approach became draining for Colin and frustrating for Ken. He commented to a friend back in California, "Although the adjustment to Midwest winters is hard, even harder to handle is the 'chill' of the community. I find myself unwilling to take the risk and share who I really am."

After his first year, Colin found that he had lost his enthusiasm for his job; it was difficult to stay focused, and his clients were less than impressed with his work. "The job itself is a great opportunity, but frankly the personal dynamics are taking their toll. Joel has been a good boss to work for, but during my job performance review, he told me that I have not impressed clients the way he had expected me to. I know I am capable of better and that I need to seriously step it up in order to survive here." Currently, he and Ken are discussing the possibility of moving back to California to start a small business together.

REFLECTION QUESTIONS

- How might Colin have more effectively anticipated and managed his move?
- If he chooses to stay, what would Colin need to do differently to make things work for himself and Ken?
- Would you advise Colin to leave his career and move back to California to start a small business with Ken? Why or why not?

ANALYSIS AND RECOMMENDATIONS

Leaving a comfortable environment where you have established connections and a support network and moving to new community is a huge challenge on many levels. It can be especially difficult when you are different in some way from the majority culture in the new environment. Colin should have anticipated those differences more thoroughly than he did. Although he assumed it would be a big change, he didn't do much research about the culture at corporate headquarters or plan how he might get support to acclimate himself to the new office. He also doesn't seem to have considered what steps might be necessary to make the move easier for Ken.

Understandably, the absence of a strong gay and lesbian network made it feel risky for Colin to reveal much about himself. However, he missed some opportunities to build a few key relationships that might have eased his transition. Patricia, his mentor and "buddy," reached out to him, but Colin did little to nurture or sustain the relationship. Since Colin felt he had a good relationship with Joel, he might have more actively sought out his support to better integrate into the culture. Colin also assumed the difficulty in connecting with others was because of his sexual orientation, but he doesn't really know how significant a factor that was. He could have been more proactive in seeking out the colleagues who would be welcoming—and used those relationships as bridges to others in the work group.

Colin was probably wise to be initially discreet about his sexual orientation until he had more information about how others were likely to react. However, by not creating a plan to build comfort and trust with others, and withdrawing from potential relationships, Colin widened the divide between his personal and professional life. That, in turn, affected his enthusiasm for the new job and, ultimately, his performance.

Colin will have to decide whether it's realistic for him to overcome the challenges of this situation. He might decide that it is not in his best interests to pursue a long-term career with the company if the culture really isn't open to his sexual orientation. However, it's likely that he can still reach out to Patricia and Joel for support and actively build relationships with his colleagues. He can work with Ken to identify some strategies to help him connect to the community. To the extent that he can take the risk to be more open with others, he will be better able to broaden and expand his base of allies beyond his gay and lesbian networks and have more control over his career choice.

THE BROADER APPLICATION

When you anticipate and actively manage the inevitable challenges of any stretch opportunity, you are more likely to be prepared to respond effectively to the obstacles you encounter. Take control of the quality of your environment, rather than letting it control you. Decisions that are rooted in moving toward a goal (such as building relationships) boost your self-esteem and sense of control more than decisions that are based on fear and avoidance (for example, Colin's potential move back to California).

Anticipate and Manage the Obstacles

As you advance in an organization, the odds increase that you will be one of the few—or the only one—"like you" in the senior ranks. Nevertheless, I encourage you to avoid playing it safe for the sake of the comforts of a familiar group or geographic location. You can navigate a transition well if you assume there will be obstacles you need to anticipate and manage—and allies who are willing to offer support and guidance.

Consider the challenges you will face in a new role or different office. What resources are available in the organization or the community to support the move? What new resources might the company be willing to put in place? How will your lifestyle be different in a new location? What will you need to do to make that lifestyle one you can sustain for a period of time? What will your family require? How can you help them make the adjustments required?

The more thought you give in advance to managing the circumstances of a career move, the more likely it is that you will be successful in spite of the challenges.

Build Relationships Strategically

Regardless of the difference that makes you a minority—race, gender, ethnicity, or sexual orientation—fear of rejection by your coworkers and a lack of personal alignment with the culture of the work environment can result in your being a different person in your work life than in your personal life. It might feel safer in the short term to hide much of yourself in your professional environment, but it tends to be draining and stifle creativity in the long run. You spend much of your energy deciding what to expose of yourself and what to protect. You tend to hold back your ideas and point of view.

> Taking the risk to be yourself frees you up to offer the full value of who you are.

Although you will sometimes encounter rejection and bias when you open yourself up to others, taking the risk to be yourself frees you up to offer the full value of who you are. Remember the Efficacy principle: it's not the stimulus, it's the response.

Strategically consider which relationships will be critical to develop in order to be effective in the work that you do. Like everyone who is somehow different from those around them, you have probably already developed a range of skills that will serve you well as you make the effort to be more genuine at work. You've learned how to assess who is likely to be open to you. You have probably developed a certain flexibility to interact in a variety of cultures. Use those skills to take a higher degree of risk in expanding your comfort with others—and their comfort with you. After you establish some initial connections, leverage the support of these individuals to reach out to others with whom establishing a relationship is more challenging.

RESILIENCE IN THE FACE OF ADVERSITY

Four years ago, Marcus was hired to head up the organization's staff recruitment and employee development function because he had a track record of creating high-performance teams that delivered strong outcomes. From the outset, Marcus invested an enormous amount of time and energy elevating his team's skill sets, empowering them to solve problems, and building a positive departmental brand and solid network. As a result, two years ago Marcus was promoted to vice president of human resources and reported directly to Travis, the chief operating officer.

On a recent Monday, Marcus was called into a meeting with Kate, the CEO, during which she explained, "Our organization will be downsizing, and this will have consequences for each of us in executive leadership roles. Instead of having both a CEO and a COO, I will assume a combined position as president and CEO. Travis, our current COO, will shift back to senior vice president, a position that will encompass both your current job as well as that of another vice president."

Kate wanted Marcus to become head of External Affairs, a role that had been discussed for the past two years but remained undefined and unfilled. Recent changes in the political landscape at the state level had created a renewed and strong business case for expanding and finally filling the position. Although he would still report to Travis, Marcus would no longer be a vice president and would have no direct reports. And due to the change in level and the need to achieve some pay equity across the organization, he would be asked to take a projected 25 percent pay cut.

Marcus confided to his mentor, "Because of the extensive scope of the role Kate described, I was able to get her to concede that we would need some additional conversation about the cut in salary. But as I was leaving her office, Kate mentioned that they would be willing to negotiate a severance if what they offered was not amenable to me. When she put that on the table, I had the sense that she was not open to negotiating salary, and they wanted me to leave. I don't want to presume this, but I have to consider all scenarios. In my entire career, I've never been in such a position. I left that meeting with a lot of negative emotions. I was shocked, hurt, sad, angry, scared, and feeling sorry for myself. I wondered if I had done something wrong and they were choosing to downgrade my position. I was tempted to quit on the spot."

Fortunately, Marcus didn't wallow in his negative emotions and self-talk. That same evening over dinner, his mentor listened and asked the right questions to help Marcus push past the emotions and identify strategies to move himself forward. To be prepared for leaving the organization, he should update his resume. To position himself within the

> Negative emotions in the face of difficulty are normal, but don't wallow in them.

organization, he should begin gathering the information needed to help craft the new position and salary range.

The next day, Marcus leveraged his network to collect information about salaries for similar positions; he found the range was $85,000 to $125,000. Armed with that data, he realized there might be enough justification to stay at his current salary level if he could shape this new position to include responsibility for the team of researchers and lobbyists employed by the organization—oversight he knew the organization felt they needed.

With coaching from his mentor, Marcus drafted a follow-up e-mail to the CEO.

> *Dear Kate,*
>
> *Thank you for taking the time on Monday to discuss the upcoming changes in the organization and provide your perspective on the implications of these changes. Travis and I are set to meet at the end of the week to shape a framework and job description for the External Affairs role. I have some thoughts as to how we can shape this position to bring maximum value to the organization.*
>
> *I appreciate your willingness to review comparable salaries for the role. This will provide us with a starting point to reach common ground on salary and inform my decision making as to whether to stay or discuss severance, which you mentioned could be made available. As we move forward in this process, it would be helpful if you could confirm timelines for finalizing the salary and any other aspects of this new role you think necessary.*

Finally, allow me to thank you for what has been a great growth opportunity as vice president of human resources. Over the past two years, our department has developed important skills and resources in both technical and people management. As a result, HR is well positioned to effectively support our organization through the upcoming challenges of this downsizing.

I look forward to our follow-up conversation.

Sincerely,
Marcus

Surprisingly, the next day Kate caught Marcus on his way to lunch: "I was very pleased to get your e-mail this morning. I feel good about what you had to say and how proactively you are moving this forward with a realistic yet positive attitude. The quality I appreciate most in you is your resiliency in the face of difficulty and change. How you handle adversity says even more to me about your character than your track record of success. I truly hope we can make this work. I would hate to lose you."

REFLECTION QUESTIONS

- In the face of adversity Marcus experienced some initial thoughts and emotions that cause some people to fall into a downward spiral. How do you imagine that he thought about this situation in order to stay resilient and focused on problem solving?
- What actions did Marcus take that were effective in responding to this challenging situation?
- What had Marcus done over the past few years that positioned him to be able to respond so effectively to the downsizing?

ANALYSIS AND RECOMMENDATIONS

Marcus clearly demonstrated intellectual and emotional resiliency in the face of adversity. It's natural to experience the range of negative emotions that Marcus initially felt. However, Marcus wasn't paralyzed by them or pulled into a helpless downward spiral. He didn't isolate himself; he didn't act impulsively. Instead, he reached out to a mentor for advice and support. With the help of his mentor, Marcus was able to refocus himself and interact in a positive manner to address the challenge. Rather than accept either of the two options he was offered (take a demotion with a pay cut or leave with a severance package), he was able to identify an option that was more to his liking: a new position with a comparable salary.

After he became clear about the outcome he wanted, Marcus used his knowledge of the organization to navigate the situation effectively. He collected the appropriate data so he had the facts to make his case. He proposed additional responsibilities he could take on in order to justify staying at his current salary. He wrote an effective e-mail to position a face-to-face meeting. In it, he was clear about what he was looking for: an agreement on a salary and job description that would make it attractive for him to stay. He didn't assume he was entitled to his former position and salary in the face of the changing needs of the organization; instead he focused on the value he could bring moving forward. Marcus's effective use of his mentor, his track record of results, and good working relationships positioned him to be influential in shaping this situation to serve his interests—and those of the organization.

THE BROADER APPLICATION

An unexpected setback is likely to arouse negative self-talk and emotions. It's easy to blame yourself or become angry at others for creating the situation. When your emotions and negative self-talk are driving your actions, you tend to react rather than respond strategically. You might act impulsively or give up and do nothing, and either reaction is unlikely to create much momentum toward a better outcome.

Respond Strategically

In the face of adversity, reach out for support and connect with someone who can give you a different perspective and way of thinking about your situation. Don't give in to "ain't it awful . . . poor me" thinking. Focus instead on figuring out what you want as an outcome and how you will respond in order to restore a sense of control and confidence. The more options you can create for yourself, the more power you have to negotiate a result that meets your needs and that others will support.

Establish and Maintain a Strong Network

Especially in times of adversity, you need a strong network. When you encounter a difficult challenge, you often need information, resources for solving the problem, and people who can support you emotionally and strategically. Your network is something that you should be maintaining and growing throughout your career. As author and career strategist Harvey Mackay says in the title of his book, "Dig your well before you're thirsty." You can't wait until you're in need of support to start building the relationships you can count on in difficult times.

Take a fresh look at the health of your network. There should be strategic connections, breadth beyond your department and your current company, quality and depth of relationships (not just surface acquaintances), reciprocity where you give as well as receive support and influence, and a dynamic flexibility, because your priorities and career needs will change.

BURNED OUT AND GOING IT ALONE

As a store manager, Amir was attentive to the needs of each shift and made sure he was there for his staff. He often commented to friends, "My employees know that I am always available to them. No matter what time of day, they can count on me to immediately come in and help fix a problem." At company headquarters, Amir had the reputation of being a hard worker with a can-do attitude who never says no.

Amir chose to work for a large retail chain because he saw potential for upward mobility. He sought a job at this particular company because it emphasized the value of diversity and inclusion at the corporate level.

After two years with the company, Amir's strong outcomes as a store manager resulted in his being promoted to district manager. In this position, he became responsible for ten stores, each of which had revenues of $1 million to $2 million annually.

When he managed one store, Amir was able to have contact with the staff every day. However, managing ten stores spread across the greater metropolitan area made this impossible. It was difficult to visit each store regularly, much less spend the amount of time with staff that he had in the past. Building relationships and trust seemed to take forever.

Sensing his frustration, Amir's boss candidly talked with him about his store managers' perceptions: "Due to the company's recent initiative to increase diversity at leadership levels, the talk among many of your direct reports is that you were promoted to district manager only because you're a minority. They're waiting to see if you are competent and can hold your own. But don't let that get to you. You had great sales numbers as a store manager."

It really shook Amir to know that he was managing people who didn't like or trust him. He became determined to prove them wrong. Many things that he normally might have delegated to them, he did himself. As a result, he was working sixty to seventy hours a week just to keep up. The jump from managing one store to managing ten stores was overwhelming him, and he was becoming less and less confident that he had what it took to be a successful district manager.

Right before the end of the fiscal year, the national store director issued an overly ambitious goal for all markets, demanding a 10 percent increase over last year's same-store sales. Amir saw no relief in sight, and burnout was imminent. He thought to himself, "I've always had a can-do attitude and have never given up, but I just don't see how I can work any more hours than I am currently." Weighed down by this unrealistic goal, Amir immediately felt his energy flag, and his focus shifted to how out of touch corporate leadership was and the downside of working for large retail chains.

REFLECTION QUESTIONS
- What might be some of the root causes of Amir's burnout?
- What does Amir need to do differently to improve his effectiveness in working with his staff?
- How should he approach the 10 percent increase in his revenue targets?

ANALYSIS AND RECOMMENDATIONS

Amir has taken on a new position, but he has not adopted a new way of operating. Even as a store manager, he spent his energy "fixing the problems." He developed a reputation as someone who got things done and produced excellent results. However, his success as a store manager was based too heavily on what he alone could accomplish. His approach to his work didn't suit his hard-won promotion with its expanded responsibilities.

Choosing not to delegate shows a lack of trust in people's skills and experience.

Amir's desire to prove himself to his direct reports exacerbated the self-imposed pressure to do it all himself. In addition, choosing not to delegate showed a lack of trust in his people's skills and experience and made Amir less effective as a district manager. This fed his team's doubts about his expertise, which is making Amir less confident in his role.

Although it can be a bit daunting to give up day-to-day control and trust that others will handle situations and meet the same high standards, Amir needs to focus on developing his staff's independence. He could begin by instituting a set of guidelines to help his staff know when to involve him, which would ensure accountability for meeting his expectations. Over time, he could expand their confidence and expertise by letting them handle certain problems without his involvement and then report the outcomes in their regular touch-base meetings. He could also outline the situations where they should bring him into the loop immediately. Typically these would be situations that require unusual budget expenditures or that might have ramifications beyond the immediate store in regards to policy or customer satisfaction.

The other problem Amir has to address is the 10 percent sales increase. He doesn't really know whether that's an achievable goal; it certainly doesn't seem so at this point. Amir needs to figure out the percentage he feels is a realistic but challenging goal. Is it 5 percent or 7 percent? Instead of focusing his energy on what he perceives to be an unrealistic goal, he should commit himself to taking the steps required to hit a goal he is confident is a stretch, but achievable.

Focusing his energy on an incremental goal does two things. First, it keeps his attention directed on what he can do rather than what he can't do. Second, by staying engaged in stretching his organization's sales revenue, he gets exposed to new information and new possibilities. He gets to see which strategies are increasing sales and which ones aren't. It's possible that the results of his efforts to hit the moderate risk target he set for himself will open up strategies for hitting the 10 percent target he originally thought was unrealistic. And if it doesn't, Amir will have data to back up the merits of the increase he did accomplish.

THE BROADER APPLICATION

In the trajectory of most careers, technical expertise—being the doer—is the driver of early success. You're known as someone who can get things done. For this, you are rewarded with a bigger span of control and the opportunity to be responsible for getting more things done. At this point, you need to make a dramatic shift in *how* you get things done.

Change the Way You Contribute

Your accomplishments can no longer be the result of your individual efforts. Rather, your accomplishments need to come from contributing through others—developing others' capabilities to solve problems and deliver quality work. To hold on to being a doer is a recipe for burnout for most people—just like it was for Amir. The relative importance of your technical expertise must decline over time and be replaced by the expertise to get work done through others. You might still know a lot about the topic, but your biggest impact will come from your relational and influence skills—the connections you can make and the resources and staff you can bring to bear on a problem.

Set Moderate Goals and Improve Incrementally

Consider how you respond when you have been given a stretch assignment that seems out of reach. Too often, we spend our time focused on what seems unrealistic about the expectations, rather than figuring out what might be attainable. You can always bring better energy to a situation when you focus on what you *can do* rather than what you *can't do*. Mace Vaughan, a longtime Efficacy trainer, says, "You can preoccupy yourself or you can occupy yourself."

When facing an unrealistic set of expectations, break the ultimate goal down into manageable steps. Focus first on a target that seems achievable in the short run—not a sure thing, but a goal that requires a level of stretch that feels possible to attain with committed, focused, and effective effort. The very process of improving yourself and your results teaches you new skills and opens up new possibilities for reaching your goal. You can then apply that new learning to push out your efforts that much further. Often, the goal that initially seemed unrealistic becomes attainable.

You will need to take some risks. You will need to be willing to work hard. You will need to pay attention to the feedback you receive about how to improve your effort. However, when you lean into learning rather than being afraid that the goal is unattainable, it's often surprising what is possible.

Focus on Influence, Not Friendships

Managing people who do not like or trust you adds a layer of complexity to your role as a leader. When you know you are perceived to be different, you might have a higher need to be liked and accepted.

It is important to have good working relationships; it is important to build trust. But effective, trusting interactions are different from friendships. When we focus on being liked, we can undermine our effectiveness to lead and manage. Our colleagues and direct reports need to be held to high standards. They need to take responsibility for meeting those standards, even when it's inconvenient or requires work they don't particularly enjoy. They might need to hear tough feedback. If we're worried about being liked, we can avoid these uncomfortable situations or fail to delegate appropriately.

As a leader, it's likely that there will always be some individuals who are unhappy or critical of your approach. You have to focus on getting results, not making friends. Trust that your respect for others and your effectiveness in getting things done will ultimately translate into respect for you—and that's what counts most.

INFLUENCING A
TOUGH SITUATION

Darnell was a well-liked 29-year-old manager in charge of sourcing diverse suppliers for a global manufacturing company. He was good at his job and conscientiously built strong relationships and networks, both internally and externally, which added to his success and credibility.

Over the past eighteen months, the company has grown aggressively and managed to capture a significantly larger share of the market. This in turn has increased its demands on its suppliers. Darnell's role in establishing and maintaining solid partnerships with key vendors was now critical to the company's sustaining its competitive advantage.

Recently, Darnell found himself stuck squarely in the middle of a contentious disagreement between the company and a longtime supplier. The company was upset that the vendor did not deliver on a few critical specifications and that the product's quality had been inconsistent in the past nine months. The supplier's complaint was that the company had abruptly changed its supply chain expectations in ways that caused it significant additional expense and seriously undermined its profit margins.

Each side was blaming the other for missed deadlines and compromised revenue streams.

The level of animosity was intense. Both parties were on the brink of walking away from the relationship, which Darnell believed would be a serious mistake for both sides. For the company, sourcing new suppliers and getting them geared up for full production was a very lengthy process, which would hamper the company's planned growth. For the supplier, walking away from this longtime account would be a huge loss of revenue.

> Choosing to influence represents a risk—and a tremendous opportunity to build credibility and expand your impact.

Instead of letting things continue to erode, Darnell made a decision to solve the problem. Leveraging the credibility and trust he had garnered with each side, he set up a meeting for the key decision makers to meet face-to-face. He knew that choosing to influence this situation represented a significant risk for him as a young manager. The parties at the table would all be at the senior vice president level or higher. Darnell would have no hierarchical authority. How he handled this meeting would either solidify—or destroy—his credibility with the company.

Darnell also knew that if he didn't do something in advance of this meeting, both sides would likely spend it finger-pointing and not make any headway. Darnell spent the week prior to the meeting talking one-on-one with key decision makers on each side, focusing on the things that he knew would bring each person to the table. During these discussions, he listened carefully, making sure he understood the issues that were most important to each side and where they might be willing to compromise.

Although he couldn't promise any solutions at this point, he made sure all the people involved knew he had heard their concerns.

He also deliberately positioned himself to be the lead negotiator. Darnell told the executives from his company, "I've been the one working most closely with this supplier, so I know the issues. I have developed a reasonable level of trust with the key folks, and they will listen if the concerns are broached in the right way."

With the supplier, he positioned himself as an ally: "I'm the best friend you've got at the table, so direct your questions and concerns to me during the meeting. You can trust that I am committed to working toward an outcome that will benefit both sides."

At the meeting, Darnell opened by painting the vision of mutual gain. He clearly articulated how each side was integral to the potential future success of the other. The company would become the supplier's largest customer and provide them with market share they never had before. Likewise, the supplier had technological capacity that the company lacked. The company could provide better service and grow its brand faster with access to the supplier's capabilities than it could on its own.

Every time the meeting started to veer off toward blaming the other side for a problem, Darnell brought it back with the question, "So what can we do to move forward?" He constantly reminded them of the benefits of a positive outcome if they could stay focused on the future. As he told his manager later, "I kept highlighting the potential gains that a restored relationship offered, and I kept reminding them why they had entered into a partnership in the first place. At times I felt like I was doing marriage counseling."

The meeting was a huge success. Each side secured agreements that resolved its most critical issues, and both sides committed to keep working on the points they were unable to resolve that day. Additionally, the company and vendor took major steps toward restoring the relationship and rebuilding trust, and both sides went away optimistic that they could make this work long term.

Looking back on his experience, Darnell commented to a mentor, "That was the biggest professional risk I've taken in my career so far. I chose to influence the outcome, and I facilitated a win-win for both parties. The risk paid off big time. It elevated my visibility and credibility within the organization, and it shaped my personal brand as a mover and shaker."

REFLECTION QUESTIONS

- Prior to the meeting, what did Darnell do well to position himself as someone who could engineer such a strong outcome?
- What did he do well during the meeting?
- How did Darnell leverage the strength of his relationships in this situation?

ANALYSIS AND RECOMMENDATIONS

Darnell didn't shrink from the challenge. He was deliberate in taking control; he assumed he could make a difference. Although he was reasonably confident he would be successful, he realized it was a big risk to facilitate an agreement and rebuild this partnership. Therefore, Darnell took an incremental approach, setting up one-on-one meetings to lay the groundwork prior to the meeting.

Darnell had already established good working relationships with both sides. He was willing to leverage the foundation of trust that he had built in order to be a credible negotiator. He positioned himself as someone who could get the parties through the conflict. He made his arguments to each person in light of what he knew about them. He was able to appeal not only to the logic of the situation but also to the more emotional interests and values that each party brought to the table.

He clearly focused the parties on what they had to gain from working through the conflict. Regardless of the obstacles, he kept the parties intent on collaboration rather than letting them get bogged down in the issues that were preventing a workable solution. He communicated a common vision to create a focus on the bigger picture.

THE BROADER APPLICATION

Darnell's approach is a great example of how to go about shaping your own circumstances and effectively influencing those around you.

Choose to Influence

Remember that influence is not asking for permission. Effective influencers assume they can shape the outcomes that are important to them—and understand that it might be a gradual process. They seldom think about whether others will let them do what they want. Rather they focus their attention on the actions required to gather the resources and support to accomplish their desired outcomes.

Build Relationships

Effective influencers always work intentionally to develop productive relationships. It is through relationships that you learn about what's important to the other parties. Your connections give you information about what compromises each side is likely to be willing to make and what they feel strongly about. Relationships are the vehicle to build trust that your interests will be protected and that you will honor the interests of others.

Be Willing to Take a Risk

There is never a guarantee that you will be successful when you choose to influence a situation. Yet without the willingness to take those kinds of risks, you will never stretch your skills or expand your base of influence. All strong influencers are willing to fail and be proven wrong. They're willing to take strong stands and can hold up under pressure and criticism.

Focus on Mutual Gains

You have to understand the interests of the people involved. What does each party see as a win? What are the shared interests? You also have to help others believe in the possibility of achieving those gains. Too often, people get bogged down in the problems and can't see the benefits that are possible. It takes someone with a strong vision of the benefits to keep the parties focused on moving forward.

Professionals who shape their own circumstances also remember that their interests are as important as the interests of others. Although they're willing to be flexible and compromise for the sake of the common good, they don't abdicate their own needs. They represent their desired outcomes respectfully but firmly.

Match Your Approach to the Situation

There is no one way to be effective when you choose to influence a situation. Those who are effective in shaping the opinions and actions of others develop a broad repertoire of strategies. They use logic and data. They appeal to emotional interests. They are willing to bargain. Or they create a shared vision. They call on the strength of the relationship. They are willing to be flexible in order to meet the needs of the situation. They realize that all influence requires some give and take, so they keep their focus on achieving what's most important.

AFTERWORD

Looking back over my life and career, I have to laugh when I remember that I almost declined the invitation to attend that Efficacy seminar thirty years ago. The experience changed my life. Dr. Jeff Howard challenged all of us to accept full responsibility for our personal and professional development. It's easy to hear his charge of "full responsibility" and miss the significance of truly adopting the mindset it implies. I encourage you to fully embrace the idea that you can produce the outcomes that are important to you through an ongoing process of development.

Wherever you are now in your lifelong journey of development, think boldly about what the future could hold for you. What have you dreamed of? Tell yourself that you can—you will—make your vision a reality. Remember that effective effort is required to promote the confidence and development that will enable you to reach your goals. Step out of your comfort zone and shape your circumstances. Don't let others dictate who you are or what you could become. Managing a meaningful career is never easy, but you will have more energy and a greater sense of control when you actively choose how you will engage in the development important to reaching your goals. Choosing to manage your life by design gives you strength. It draws you forward. It focuses you on the possibilities rather than the limitations.

> Efficacy is the power to produce a desired effect. It is a set of thoughts and behaviors that give you the highest return on the investment of your time and effort.

Learn from your mistakes. Understand that no matter how determined you are or how much courage you bring, there will be setbacks. Don't let yourself be sidelined by difficulties or temporary failures. Use the feedback from your efforts to craft a better approach and keep moving toward your ultimate goal.

Surround yourself with people who will support your development. Build a community that understands what you're about and will create forward momentum for you to get where you want to go. Seek out those who will feed your confidence and your effective effort, especially during times when you are vulnerable to the impact of external challenges.

The principles of Efficacy gave me a way to nurture ongoing development—to shape my effort and build my capacity to influence my career through an incremental process. I firmly hope these principles do for you what they did for me.

We ask ourselves, Who am I to be brilliant, gorgeous, talented, fabulous? Actually, who are you not *to be? . . . Your playing small doesn't serve the world . . . . As we let our own light shine, we unconsciously give other people permission to do the same. As we're liberated from our own fear, our presence automatically liberates others.*

—Marianne Williamson, *A Return to Love* (1992)